Second Edition

Science
Workshop

Reading,

Writing,

and

Thinking

Like a

Scientist

How I grew in my egg

Wendy Saul

Jeanne Reardon • Charles Pearce • Donna Dieckman • Donna Neutze

HEINEMANN
Portsmouth, I

Heinemann
A division of Reed Elsevier Inc.
361 Hanover Street
Portsmouth, NH 03801–3912
www.heinemann.com

Offices and agents throughout the world

The authors and publisher wish to thank those who have generously given permission to reprint borrowed material:
Figures 3–4, 3–7, 3–8, 3–10, 3–11, 3–12 and 6–1 are reprinted from *Nurturing Inquiry: Real Science for the Elementary Classroom* by Charles R. Pearce. Copyright © 1999 by Charles R. Pearce. Published by Heinemann, a division of Reed Elsevier Inc., Portsmouth, NH. Reprinted by permission of the author and publisher.

Tables 6–1, 6–2, and 6–3 are reprinted from the paper "The Science–Literacy Connection: A Case Study of the Valle Imperial Project in Science, 1995–1999" by Michael P. Klentschy presented at Crossing Borders: Connecting Science and Literacy Conference, Baltimore, MD, in August 2001. Reprinted by permission of Michael P. Klentschy.

Library of Congress Cataloging-in-Publication Data
Science workshop : reading, writing, and thinking like a scientist / Wendy Saul . . . [et al.].—2nd ed.
     p. cm.
Includes bibliographical references.
  ISBN 0-325-00510-9 (pbk. : alk. paper)
 1. Science—Study and teaching (Elementary)—United States.
2. Language experience approach in education—United States.
3. Teaching—Aids and devices. I. Saul, Wendy.
 LB1585.3 .S36 2002
 372.3'5'044—dc21

                                                        2002005927

Editor: Robin Najar
Production: Lynne Reed
Cover design: Night & Day Design
Cover illustration: Emma Tobin
Typesetter: Argosy
Manufacturing: Steve Bernier

Printed in the United States of America on acid-free paper
06   05   04   03   02   VP   1   2   3   4   5

For Susan Snyder, a critical friend to us all.

Contents

Acknowledgments

This material is based on work supported by the National Science Foundation under Grant No. 9912078. Any opinions, findings, and conclusions or recommendations expressed in this material are those of the author(s) and do not necessarily reflect the views of the National Science Foundation.

Contributors

Wendy Saul, Professor of Education at the University of Maryland, Baltimore County (UMBC), teaches courses on literacy, the study of teaching, and nonfiction for children and adolescents. She is editor of *Thinking Classroom: An International Journal of Reading, Writing and Critical Reflection* published by the International Reading Association and author/editor of a number of books about the science–literacy connection, including *Vital Connections: Children, Science, and Books* (Heinemann 1991) and *Beyond the Science Kit* (Heinemann 1996). As director of the National Science Foundation-supported "Elementary Science Integration Projects," she has a special interest in helping educators create reading and writing activities that inform and are informed by science. She is also the originator of *Search It! Science: The Books You Need at Lightning Speed* (searchit.heinemann.com), a computer program that suggests appropriate science titles for young readers, their teachers, and librarians.

Jeanne Reardon has been teaching for thirty years in Montgomery County, Maryland, a large public school district outside Washington, DC. Her articles about literacy, critical reflection, and science have been published nationally in *The New Advocate* and internationally in *Thinking Classroom*. She has contributed chapters to *Vital Connections: Children, Science, and Books* (Heinemann 1991), *Beyond the Science Kit: Inquiry in Action* (Heinemann 1996), the first edition of *Science Workshop* (Heinemann 1993), and *Assessment & Evaluation for Student-Centered Learning* (Christopher Gordon 1994). In 1993, Reardon received the Presidential Award for Excellence in Science Teaching.

Donna Dieckman, program director for the Elementary Science Integration Projects at the University of Maryland, Baltimore County (UMBC), works with classroom teachers, administrators, and university researchers on programs designed to support science and literacy connections. During her nine years as a classroom teacher, she became a strong advocate of using children's literature in the classroom. She has served as a member of the National Science Teacher's Association–Children's Book Council joint panel that selects the Outstanding Science Tradebook

Awards in children's literature. She contributed a chapter to *Beyond the Science Kit: Inquiry in Action* (Heinemann 1996).

Charles Pearce is a teacher at Manchester Elementary School in Manchester, Maryland, and the recipient of the President's Award for Excellence in Science Teaching. Pearce is a lead teacher for the Elementary Science Integration Projects and a frequent presenter at regional and national conferences and workshops for teachers. He is the inspiration for the Kids' Inquiry Conference (KIC), which he has spearheaded for the past ten years, and is the author of *Nurturing Inquiry: Real Science for the Elementary Classroom* (Heinemann 1999).

Donna Neutze, project coordinator for the Elementary Science Integration Projects at the University of Maryland, Baltimore County (UMBC), oversees the daily operations of *Search It! Science,* a database of more than 3,000 outstanding children's science books, and she coordinates the Kids Inquiry Conference (KIC). She teaches a course in Adolescent Literature at UMBC and contributes web columns for *Thinking Classroom,* a publication of the International Reading Association. She is currently enrolled in a PhD program in Language, Literacy and Culture, pursuing her research interests in nonfiction children's literature and gender-related issues.

1 *Science Workshop*

Wendy Saul

Washington, DC, 1987: Susan Snyder, a grants officer from the National Science Foundation, agreed to talk with me about people I privately called *genius teachers*. Here was my idea: In elementary schools, at least, there are practitioners who do a spectacular job of teaching whatever topic is set before them. It is not simply that these educators are energetic or responsive in their delivery—although surely they are—but rather that they are somehow able to find the intellectual kernel that could be used to seed instruction and engage students in rigorous, satisfying academic work. Most of these teachers now focus on literacy instruction, I told Susan, but that is largely because it is in the literacy world that they find the most interesting conversations about teaching taking place. What if we could interest these folks in science? What could they teach us about how students come to better understand the physical world?

Susan thought hard about this proposition. "I know 'genius teachers,' too" she began, "but part of what makes them 'genius' is their knowledge of subject matter. They get it—what it means to ask good questions about outer space or how a bee flies. Their insight comes from immersion in the content. They have a clear idea of how what a student knows connects to fundamental scientific principles, a more robust understanding of science itself."

Good teaching, we both realized, engages students and their teachers in both process and content.

Washington, DC, 1999: As coordinator of an international project based largely in Eastern Europe, Central Europe, and Central Asia, I get to visit lots of schools from the Baltic Sea to the Caspian Sea. These are countries that historically have done well on the TIMMS test, countries with a high basic literacy rate. Why, then, have they invited in *experts* from the West to introduce new teaching methods?

Sitting in classrooms the answer becomes clear. Although these teachers are clearly adept at teaching the factual knowledge that enables students to test well, critical thinking, active learning, and opportunities for decision making are too often absent. The teachers in this region, as well as their government officials, wonder how students will be able to make their way in a world that calls on citizens to do more than reproduce factual information.

For a Westerner, the level of control I observe is surprising. I visit a group of students who were directed to use catalog information to order a product and then write a letter of complaint, saying that the wrong goods were sent. It's a good assignment that is likely to produce lively writing. The first letter sends me into gales of appreciative laughter. The boy has written about a suit that is the wrong size, a shirt that is the wrong color, and another article of clothing that does not match the catalog description. Then the second student reads. It is the same letter with the color of the shirt changed. Then a third student reads . . . the same letter with another very minor change. Finally, I realize that the assignment had been so carefully structured and delineated that the letters would differ only in minute detail. "But weren't students doing it correctly?" asks the teacher in charge.

Baltimore, MD, 2001: The reports are beginning to surface: Some schools are so worried about their reading scores that they have started to replace hands-on science programs with textbook-based curricula, ostensibly to reinforce literacy skills. When feeling particularly under the gun, science is dropped completely in favor of work in reading.

And all too often, the reading instruction offered is largely scripted, relying on drill and rote recall. Texts are written specifically so that students can practice their decoding skills and little attention is devoted to meaning-making and those understandings that bring readers back to books and words again and again.

I visit a state-level administrator and ask about this seeming preoccupation with decoding, "Why are critical thinking and meaning-making ignored rather than taught alongside decoding skills?"

His reply: "They should be but . . ."

There are several problems, as I understood his analysis. The first is that many educators see skills instruction as preceding work in critical thinking—if students can't decode, how are they going to do something even more difficult? From what we know from both experience and the literature, this is patently untrue.

A second problem is that teaching decoding is seen as more doable, or easier, than teaching thinking. In an era of testing, purveyors of this new curriculum believe that they can show gains of basic skills on tests much more easily than they can show gains in thinking. An aligned problem is that there are few tests that measure critical thinking and performance-based outcomes. In Maryland, however, we were fortunate to have such a test, although its power was somewhat diminished because it was used only to evaluate school improvement and the buy-in from individual parents was not fully apparent. I worry that the approach taken even in this region is, however, to drill letters and sounds for two years and then panic in the third grade when performance assessment is first given.

A third problem has to do with the *state* of schools today. Although the professional literature overflows with advice on *best practices*, the testing may, in reality, serve as an attempt to combat *worst practices*. Surely, no one wants to see inadequate teaching, and the results of poor instruction are devastating for children. But I worry that in trying to combat worst practices, we leave little time or space for something better. I also worry about the profession—what opportunities are there for good, creative, smart educators to practice their art?

Also, of course, the most important issue has to do with student learning. The highly regarded literacy scholar James Gee notes that "more children fail in school, in the long run, because they cannot cope with 'academic language' than because they cannot decode print." Here Gee is not talking about a list of vocabulary words germane to an academic discipline, but rather about a way of thinking, talking, and working that people within that discipline can recognize as their own. He wants students to learn how to approach problems and to find ways to share their questions and understandings and critical reflections with others who are schooled in this discipline.

Gee's point, and one I strongly subscribe to, is that literacy skills are best taught—perhaps can only really be taught—in context. One engages in science-related reading and writing as one does science. To put it differently, it is in the doing of science, not just in reading about it, that students learn to master the concepts that will enable them to better understand both the reading and writing of expository and procedural text. To teach science reading and writing and talk about it without hands-on work makes as much sense as learning to play the piano on a paper keyboard.

There is a lot of good news here. Students will surely find contextualized literacy more engaging. Plus, in terms of what they learn, the material will be more meaningful and more intellectually challenging; intellectual opportunities for teachers and children abound in classrooms such as those described in this book. The case we make here is for science–literacy connections, although it can certainly be applied to other disciplines. We are unabashedly enthusiastic about this work in science because the thinking that is invited through science can easily and meaningfully be transferred to other areas, just as certain language skills from other disciplines can be transferred to and used in science. For instance, students' work in science provides them with powerful examples of cause and effect. This understanding may be useful as they seek evidence to create arguments in favor of or against other propositions that have nothing to do with science per se. As one seeks ways to talk about one's work in science, young practitioners naturally seek and use a vocabulary and a discourse that educated adult practitioners use as they seek to communicate both orally and in print about the information they have gleaned.

The Science Workshop, as it is described in this book, offers young people opportunities to act in a world in which information is shared and revised and in which critical evaluation is considered a necessary tool for survival. The workshop model pushes both teachers and students past *minimum competence*. Many pioneering teachers, at various points in history, have figured out ways to do more than the minimum required and to expect more from children than recitation. The usual strategy, and one that the teachers whose essays appear in this book illustrate, is to move a parallel *thinking* curriculum right in beside the more traditional textbook-based, scripted programs. Here is a reason for teachers to stay in the profession, because as practitioners they find satisfaction in helping children think hard, explore, investigate, and grow as independent learners.

But what do we mean by a Science Workshop?* Let's look at my observation notes. Here is a description of a classroom in which a tenacious teacher who values thinking and sustained engagement encourages her students.

> Walking into the sixth-grade area, it is difficult to spot her. Finally I find the teacher, belly down on the carpeted floor, watching with three children as mealworms scurry in a shoebox. "Which colors do they like?" asks one youngster. After listening to a three-minute discussion on "how you tell," the teacher interrupts with a question: "When you set up this experiment, how will you decide whether the mealworms are being given a *fair trial*?" Seeing that the discussion is again underway, she jots something on a sticky note and moves on to talk with a girl who is looking at a live frog and comparing it with the glossy, color photograph in the trade book she holds.
>
> "Ms. Reeves, this frog doesn't look the same as the one in the picture."
>
> "Good observation," the teacher replies. "Why not make a list of all the differences you notice?"
>
> The teacher proceeds from group to group, stopping to chat with individuals, taking an occasional note. Only two of the groups are working with the same materials; one group is helping prove a *theory* that

---

*We, the authors of this book, have been influenced by the Writing Workshop model first introduced by Donald Graves, Lucy Calkins, Nancie Atwell and others. We have revised, modified and added to these ideas, reshaping them for the teaching of science. For this reason, we use initial capital letters in referring to the Science Workshop as a constellation of the specific ideas we propose. When using the term in a more general sense, lower case (science workshop) was used.

another group has decided is ready to be tested elsewhere. My over-whelming sense, as an observer, is that this classroom is a busy place.

After allowing the students about thirty minutes for investigation, the teacher gives a five-minute warning, reminding them to log in the day's activities. The class is then told they will meet to discuss the science activities right after lunch.

This is good teaching, which honors content knowledge and process knowledge. It begins where children are—it takes them as they come—and moves them to a better academic place. Such classes invite students who wish to dwell on a topic time for reflection and further investigation. This kind of teaching gives children who are slower to catch on time to talk with those who *get it* and to ask how they *got it*. The teacher's goal is not to improve test scores—although that often happens—but rather to attend to her students' intellectual journeys, that is, to consider where students have been and to guide them to where they are headed.

The class just described is an example of what we call a *Science Workshop*. What makes it a workshop? What makes one workshop like another? Why was the term *workshop* borrowed from the literacy community, and what does a *science* workshop have in common with its literacy counterparts? How does one go about organizing a workshop? What principles undergird instruction and planning? This book is designed to help answer these questions. It also asks readers to think about thinking. The Science Workshop, in this sense, serves as the keystone where investigations and literacy work meet. The approach asks students and their teachers to engage as problem solvers.

Characterizing a Workshop

A Science Workshop certainly looks different for different grades in different locales, and surely the passions of the teacher and the children in her charge will make one year different from the next. Still, as we think back, the workshop embodies three important elements: authenticity, autonomy, and community.

Authenticity

Authenticity is a critical element in any workshop model. A good science workshop needs to foster the kind of thinking engaged in by scientists, those people who find pleasure in the systematic study of our world. As such, an understanding of what scientists do—how they ask questions, explore phenomena, speculate about why certain things happen, and arrive at convincing and reasonable answers—needs to be an essential piece of any science workshop. A general understanding of these processes is well within the grasp of elementary school teachers and their students.

Authenticity should also be a feature of the subjects to be investigated. Children need to be working on problems that they recognize as personally challenging and that make sense to them in the world in which they operate. Although teachers or books may be instrumental in generating an initial interest in a topic, students must play a major role in determining the path for pursuing that inquiry.

Those familiar with the power of literature to nurture reading and writing abilities can appreciate how children seek to understand the way the world works, both as lovers of knowledge and as participants in experiments that result in satisfying explanations. Science trade books—literature that tells stories about scientific events, recounts and explains facts, or proposes activities—offer another authentic science voice in the classroom.

Authenticity is also evident in the way workshop teachers and children relate to one another. Children's ideas are respected and credited, and, in the best lessons, teachers and children share their curiosities. Workshop talk feels more like a professional meeting than the kind of parroting and cajoling dialogue that results when students are asked to guess the answer the teacher wants. This is not to suggest that such formats are never in teaching science, but we need to recognize that teacher-centered and teacher-controlled lessons are not components of process-oriented workshops.

Autonomy

Autonomy is another feature that characterizes the workshop. Student scientists, like their professional counterparts, take on both the freedom and the responsibilities associated with trying to produce convincing arguments and data-rich explanations. In this sense there are many decisions to be made: Given the general parameters established by the teacher, how will I go about my work? with whom do I wish to work? how do I know when I'm doing a good job? what do I do next? The science and writing workshops have much in common—both seek to help children become more adept at learning on their own, and more able to engage in sustained and focused thought.

The other significant feature of the Science Workshop has to do with time. Units that come prepackaged from the school district arrive and depart on specific dates. This means that children and teachers must fit their explorations into discrete and relatively short time periods. Science Workshop involves more time than the discrete science lesson, but the time it takes can also be counted as writing, reading, art, or social studies.

The authors of this book are thoroughly committed to the notion that children need time to "mess around" in science. Generally, young people benefit from repeating the same activity several times, in just the same way they enjoy reading a book or singing a song again and again.

Repeated investigation convinces children of one of the major tenets of science—the same procedure with the same materials leads to the same result. By and large, kit programs do little to encourage such repetition because it seems less efficient and economical. Textbook programs based on a single demonstration do even less in this regard.

We all need time to "worry" ideas into place. An argument could be made that *not* giving children that time may finally be our undoing. If young people are to understand that what matters most in school is reasoned analysis rather than doctrine, they need to believe in what they see and do, not take it on faith that what their teacher says is correct. Under pressure to "move on," a teacher may give up by telling children the *answer* and by having them repeat it either orally or on a test. And children, eager to please, repeat what the teacher deems worthy of a good grade. In so doing, young people learn that school is about a body of knowledge to be memorized rather than understood, and that the classroom is an arena where curiosity and persistence count for little.

Because workshop interests and plans vary, students are often engaged in a wide variety of activities. Teachers within a Science Workshop have learned to be comfortable changing gears and keeping track of such dissimilarities. Even when a project starts from a similar premise or question—Which fabric is more waterproof? What do we know about a hermit crab's claw?—diversity of response is not only expected but encouraged.

Community

A sense of community is also central to the workshop. Ideally, classrooms are places where teachers and children work as a unique community of thinkers. One year looks different from another, not just because another curriculum package is adopted on the district level, but because each year teachers and children come with new thoughts and experiences to share. To succeed in a workshop, children and teachers must be aware of the resources available in the classroom community—Who writes fantasy and who reads biography? Who spells well? Who never forgets her homework? In a workshop, children are encouraged to use each other and collaboration is invited.

Community is also evident in the standards students set for their work. Because they see themselves as practicing authors or scientists, their results are presented to and evaluated by peers. Questions, such as the one posed by teacher Jeanne Reardon ("What evidence do my first graders find convincing in evaluating data?"), become logical in a workshop environment where sharing is an ordinary and important part of the day.

There are, however, significant differences between the intellectual rules set by the science and language communities and these differences are reflected in practice. Whereas emotion is often central to literary response, in science one actively seeks to separate emotional reactions from empirical evidence. In science, if there is a choice between believing what seems entirely logical and clearly stated and believing the data—the concrete results of an experiment—it is incumbent on the science student to opt for the data. The point here is that an experiment or explanation is not valued because everyone in the class agrees that it is correct. Rather, the power of an idea is evidenced in repetition and prediction—Will it work that way every time? Can I predict which flowers these bees are more likely to visit? No one, on the other hand, would say: "This is an excellent poem because I can write one just like it." or "This book is wonderful because I knew exactly what would happen to the protagonist."

But this does *not* mean that emotion is absent from the science workshop. Children and adults can learn to appreciate skepticism in a whole-hearted way. Moreover, they can be impressed, emotionally impressed, with good questions and interesting findings. In developing hypotheses, "gut" feelings do count; there are many famous stories about scientists working doggedly on problems day in and day out only to have the solution come suddenly in a dream. The problems and solutions of science can mean enough to penetrate an investigator's subconscious; in such instances the distinctions between cognitive and affective responses become blurred. An atmosphere that supports the rethinking of ideas and invites an appreciation of problem solving is one that fosters science as well as language learning.

Cooperative learning strategies and an assigned sharing/celebration time are often regular features of the process-oriented classroom. But in a successful workshop, sharing and cooperation go far beyond the technical, sometimes formulaic, exercises designed to model caring and trust, encouragement and appreciation. Through the workshop, children and teachers seek to help one another grow, learn, and share the frustration and delight of working hard. Whereas in many classrooms children come to value others' failures as a way to buoy their own successes, in a workshop excellence and improvement are viewed as both personal and community triumphs.

In speaking primarily to the similarities between a reading/writing workshop and a science workshop, I do not wish to ignore the differences. I believe, for instance, that most teachers have a clearer understanding of the way that developmental issues are played out in the learning of language than in the learning of science. Also, while the study of reading or writing might well begin with the need for communication and students' experiences with oral language, there are many questions about how the languages of science, both linguistic and mathematical, play off one another. Further, ordinary adult language activities—reading a novel or writing a well-crafted letter—lead teachers to believe that they can teach reading and writing. However, adult science—its precision, stature, and distance from everyday experience—often leads teachers to believe that they have nothing to offer children in science. We take exception to that.

Using Ourselves

Teachers who feel insecure about teaching science generally begin by thinking how different science is from anything they know. Interestingly, the list of what they don't know tends to focus on content: I don't know about batteries. I don't know the difference between metamorphic and igneous rock. I don't know about the phases of the moon. In an attempt to empower science-phobic teachers, science educators have tended to focus on teaching content—"Here's a hands-on activity you can do with children," says the workshop leader; and teachers, eager for something that children will enjoy and learn from, leave the workshop happy. The problem, of course, is that in their hearts these teachers don't believe that what they can do is really science. They are still burdened by the weight of all they don't know and are left wondering what will happen when children need something substantive and information-based. Real science people, they believe, are a fountain of facts.

Such opinions are reinforced in various ways. Scientists and science educators regularly express something between distress and disgust about how few college science courses elementary school teachers typically take. Thinking back to that freshman biology or chemistry class, teachers ponder all the courses in which they did not enroll. Simply to keep up with the four units in the third-grade curriculum, they should have, according to some, taken courses in geology, physics, and paleontology.

Popular culture also contributes to the sense of desperation that the teacher with a meager science background feels. In a society that recognizes and values expertise, we know that scientists are the ones to turn to for specialized information and critical, informed judgments. A team of scientists is called in to discuss global warming, world hunger, the reasons the spaceship *Challenger* exploded, and so forth. Of course, these aren't the same teams of scientists, but somehow that fact isn't made clear. My husband, who has a PhD in chemistry, is an amateur astronomer, and writes about environmental issues, doesn't know enough geology to teach a standard fourth-grade unit. The difference is that he would approach the task as interesting, and he would be confident about his ability to connect what he already knows to the subject at hand.

I suspect that additional coursework, though potentially helpful, is not the key to more and better elementary school science. Nor is it in our interest to turn teachers into resource "junkies"—people in search of more and better materials and activities. Rather, if we seek real change in attitudes toward science, we need to begin with the strengths teachers have and with their ability to locate help when necessary. An example might prove useful here.

A science resource specialist in an elementary school arranged for the third graders to dissect fish, one fish per child. The activity began in the regular classroom: twenty-six children gathered around the chalkboard and the resource teacher asked them what they expected to find. Three children eagerly answered questions and another four or five seemed to be actively listening. Then the children followed the science specialist into the science room, where the fish were distributed.

The science teacher had assembled a team of adults—herself, the regular teacher, an aide, and a parent with a PhD in neuroscience. The children were divided into groups, and each adult was kept busy attending to six or seven youngsters trying to use knives. During and after all the fish were opened, the adults helped children identify gills, guts, scales, and fins.

Two teacher observers (let's call them X and Y) commented on this event, which by all accounts went well. Mr. X focused almost entirely on the kind and amount of information the science specialist and scientist had at their disposal. In this hierarchy the science teacher had the greatest knowledge, the scientist was second, the aide (a recreational fisherman) was third, and the regular teacher had the least information to share with the students. Observer X determined not only that he knew less than the classroom teacher, but also that he was put off by the slimy innards. This observation provided confirmation—living proof—that teacher/observer X would never be able to teach science.

The second observer, Ms. Y, "used" herself in her analysis. To begin, she noticed the general lack of participation in the precutting phase. As a writing teacher, Ms. Y realized that some sort of write-to-know activity—drawing a picture, making a list, or collaborating with a friend on a short discussion about what might be inside—would have involved every child in the class and set up each one to better appreciate the hands-on activity.

Second, because she and the children in her own classroom were comfortable with the idea that everyone need not be doing the same thing at the same time, Ms. Y realized that the hands-on work could have taken place in the regular classroom, thus reducing the number of adults needed to make the dissection part of the daily routine rather than a special activity.

Finally, Ms. Y felt confident that she could find trade books and reference materials that would assist her in answering children's questions, and that she didn't need to become an expert in ichthyology to undertake the dissection activity. In short, the teacher who had the confidence to use herself left the demonstration lesson ready and able to take on this activity and ones like it. The teacher awed by expertise, on the other hand, felt confirmed in his insecurity; Mr. X concluded that it was better to stay away from what he didn't know well.

This book assumes that teachers familiar with the workshop model have a great resource for building on and connecting with children's natural interest in science. The chapters that follow make some explicit procedural suggestions and show how knowledge of process in reading and writing can be used as the scaffold for helping children investigate their natural world.

What *Do* We Know?

Through the years we have learned that the best way to educate teachers is to have them engage in the same processes we advocate for students, and then to give the practitioners time to reflect on or "unpack" what they have learned. We have also come to understand that it is useful to carry the knowledge from one subject area to another. For instance, as a reading/language arts teacher, I know that I need engaging materials—books about objects, people, or experiences familiar and interesting to the children in my class as well as books that are unfamiliar and challenge children to view the world differently. Books function in different ways in classrooms: There are titles that children can read independently, and books that are best shared with a friend. I also want books that I, as a teacher, enjoy reading and books that I can use to learn along with the children. If a book becomes stale for me, I am less able to share my passion for words and ideas. I choose books with children, not for children, and as a reader/advisor, look for connections between what has interested them—subjects, authors, feelings—and the available literature. If I have read the book before, I am better able to recommend and discuss it. Even if my recommendation is "blind," I still feel comfortable asking authentic, generic questions.

That same confidence many teachers feel about reading materials needs to characterize science instruction. Often authors of textbooks or kit programs begin by focusing on the subject matter or topic. Are there certain topics that provide richer fields for exploration than others? It is important, however, to recognize that the audience for regional or national programs may be different from the particular class with a particular teacher (i.e., you).

It may make sense to begin a science workshop by focusing not on the subject, which can quickly lead away from what you know, but rather on the experiences you share with the children in your charge. Start with some local interest question—Which markers work best? What makes some balls roll faster than others? Start with concrete experience—a pray-ing mantis found on the way to school, a flower in the schoolyard that isn't immediately recognized. Start always with a curiosity or a concern, never with an abstract concept like molecules or fission that cannot be sensed and tested directly. Bernie Zubrowski (1990), children's author and a physicist by training, talks about the importance of beginning with materials that have an intrinsic interest. His own work with balloons, cars, mirrors, clocks, drinking-straw constructions, and bubbles provides a model for challenges that can be undertaken in a workshop setting.

Materials for a science workshop need not be expensive and shouldn't be hard to find. Through the years, we have developed attentive eyes and see abundant examples of science in practice—at the local hardware store, as the car mechanic troubleshoots a problem, watching the gardener who experiments with what the deer will and might not eat. But, as James Rutherford (1991), formerly chief education officer of the American Association for the Advancement of Science, has pointed out, science is not in the materials but in the perspective one takes toward those materials, in the questions one asks and answers about those materials.

> Seashells, for example, are not science; they are just things. Admiring their beauty is not science. Drawing them carefully may or may not be science depending on its purpose. Capturing their beauty is a wonderful thing to do, but it is not science. Trying to figure out things about seashells: that is science. But a child doesn't care what you call it as long as it's interesting. Do spiral shells always spiral in the same direction, or are some oriented the other way? Why? And why are some seashells found on mountaintops? Are all seashells made out of the same thing? Does it make a difference if the creatures that live in them come from saltwater or freshwater? There are endless questions. By asking ques-tions and trying to determine the answers, especially through personal investigation, children find themselves doing science without thinking it is anything out of the ordinary and gaining, eventually, a good familiar-ity with the territory. (24–25)

A confident and interested teacher models those questions and can employ the *lens* of science without becoming a subject specialist. It takes honesty, enthusiasm, and the ability to search for answers through books and exper-iments and experts, but all teachers worth their salt know how to do that.

Teachers in a science workshop take on two other very important roles. Aside from helping to identify subjects and activities that profit from investigation, it is their responsibility to (1) figure out the way the children in their charge are making sense of what they study and (2) to interject questions that will cause a child to rethink explanations that cannot be generalized.

Matthew, a second grader, was asked to take a clay ball and "see if you can find a way to make it float." A casual observer walking into the room might have seen an intense-looking little boy jabbing his pencil into a ball of clay, seemingly frustrated and "off-task." His teacher, however, knew enough to ask this youngster about his activity. "Well," explained Matthew, "I knew that anyone could float a clay raft, so I decided to make pumice stone."

Sometimes making sense of a child's explanations is simply a matter of listening. At other points, probing questions are needed. A science workshop is based on the assumption that children are seeking to make sense, to find consistencies in their world, and to understand what will enable them to predict and repeat the patterns they see. A large part of science workshop, then, exists in the mind of the teacher.

But what about children who are obviously *getting it wrong*? Matthew, for instance, will not be able to create pumice stone out of clay. It is the teacher's responsibility in these instances to try to create situations that will worry the child into rethinking the *information* or explanation. Sometimes this is done through an event. Matthew, for instance, might benefit from looking at a piece of pumice stone alongside his clay dotted with holes. In other instances, a question might suffice. If he were to report, for instance, that his pumice clay *does* float, the teacher might help the child think through a definition of what it means to float: "Do some things float better than others?"

Instead of starting with subject-matter objectives, or developmental theory, or teacher expertise, a workshop focuses on the children's increasing knowledge of the way they learn, are convinced, and convince others. These are the processes teachers and children work together to understand. But workshop teachers are not lacking in goals; rather, they assume that goals for children differ, depending on the insights and information students begin with and their developmental capacities. Workshop teachers continually look for ways that children's interests can be tied to larger scientific understandings, such as those elaborated in our science standards.

Over the years it has become clear to me that many of the children who are deemed *good* in science are those who enjoy the power of being able to name objects or events. Science workshop is designed to invite a different sort of pleasure from studying the natural world; we seek to help children develop a repertoire of strategies for addressing their own curiosities and to recognize, through experience, which questions will be clarified by which activities. Workshop teachers think of science as a lens—a pattern of thought and/or a conversation that invites even young children to wonder, to speculate, and to satisfy at least some of their own curiosities.

If young people leave their elementary schools able to characterize and make explicit what counts as evidence, to generate questions and answers that can be replicated and explained, to face the challenges of science without fear, I suspect that we will have made considerable progress. These goals are those espoused by advocates of large-scale teacher reform, especially those committed to a constructionist approach. What then is the difference between the approach advocated here and the large-scale efforts that seek to effect change?

The Politics of Education

Many classrooms today are organized according to a linear, externally controlled curriculum. *Science Workshop* represents a markedly different view of the teaching profession as well as a different view of teacher education. The intent of scope and sequence charts, lists of *essentials*, and other efforts that seek to specify required course content is to make sure (1) that there is a pattern to what children learn and (2) that minimum standards are adhered to. Ideally, such programs ensure that every student is offered an opportunity to engage in worthwhile activities. Although this is certainly a laudable goal, it addresses only the notion of minimum competence, both on the part of students and teachers. If my teacher/friend Dave Robson is right, that all this talk about "best practices" may really be an attempt to avoid "worst practices," provisions need to be made for educators who can move beyond, and can help colleagues move beyond, decision-free teaching.

When teachers feel and believe that they know little to nothing about a subject, their tendency is to avoid the subject, and make their ignorance less obvious. To combat this tendency, school districts have mandated the use of programs that are so *well-designed* that teacher ignorance is masked. I worry, however, that these comprehensive programs, coupled with teachers' insecurities, may unwittingly promote disengagement with, distance from, and disinterest in the subjects we seek to teach. Although the comprehensive programs or scope-and-sequence guides may be useful as a starting point, workshop teachers see their responsibilities as extending far beyond the minimum competence that school systems often establish as a goal.

How do workshop teachers go about expanding their science programs and building on their professional strengths? Claryce Evans of the Educator's Forum in Boston notes that, traditionally, practitioners concerned with professional growth are moved from one inservice program to another, supposedly learning new information, a new way to use materials, a new way to organize the school day, a new way to deal with parents. It is amazing how little of our professional time is spent reflecting on what we already know, building on what is already working in classrooms, and giving critical attention to what appears problematic. Although other social service professionals, such as psychologists and social workers, spend hours considering their interactions with their clients, teachers rarely find time to discuss the issues that dominate their thinking about classroom life.

Science Workshop makes an explicit attempt to build on the questions, concerns, and support networks that teachers already have in place. Science is not a time to drop all the kid-watching skills we have developed in favor of something new. At this point in history, it may be hard to find a forum dedicated to thinking about how children *learn*. Experienced elementary school teachers often voice their belief that children do not separate the world into discrete branches of knowledge that remain fixed and isolated. As teachers we need to capitalize on intellectual *crossovers*, not fight them. As students develop confidence and skill as writers and readers, we must encourage a *spillover* into science by introducing them to and helping them evaluate science trade books and websites. Science writing or expository prose represents an incredibly powerful mode of expression and procedural text is useful for activities as diverse as performing magic tricks to considering the appropriateness of a given *fair* test. Reciprocal benefits from science also accrue—the habits of mind students develop as close observers and analytic thinkers serve them well in other academic or social pursuits. The best elementary school teachers seek to foster students' wide-ranging interests and celebrate the generalist's urge to make connections in the classroom community.

Sadly, this view of knowledge is not mirrored in the professional opportunities afforded most teachers. To date, there is no national organization for educators who wish to learn more about the role of liberal arts education in the elementary schools. Truly, it is an unusual teacher or teacher/educator who is able to attend more than one professional meeting a year even though the organizations that support science (NSTA), literacy (IRA and NCTE), social studies (NCSS), and mathematics (NCTM) hold meetings at different times in different places. Perhaps the alliances among educators with interests in interdisciplinary teaching need to be forged at the grass roots, that is, initiated by teachers or administrators at individual schools or the district level.

Charles Pearce, Jeanne Reardon, and Donna Dieckman are teachers whose classrooms have changed not as the result of a new curriculum package but because of intense professional discussions and extensive reading. They have learned from and with colleagues whose insights and questions made the strange familiar and the familiar strange. They have explored, investigated, and analyzed scientific phenomena themselves so that they could understand what children engaged in schoolwork need to think about and feel and understand. The public recital of their experiences represents a commitment not only to a workshop model, but to a profession that values intelligence, community, and caring.

Although the ideas expressed on the preceding pages may appeal to educators, we recognize that, ultimately, the power of the argument advanced is in its viability as classroom practice. In this sense the heart of *Science Workshop* begins here.

References

Gee, J. P. "Language in the Science Classroom: Academic Social Languages as the Heart of School-Based Literacy." Paper presented at the Crossing Borders: Connecting Science and Literacy Conference, Baltimore, MD, August 2001.

Rutherford, F. 1991. "Vital Connections: Children, Books, and Science." In *Vital Connections: Children, Science, and Books,* edited by W. Saul and S. Jagusch. Washington, DC: Library of Congress. (Reprinted by Heinemann Educational Books, Portsmouth, NH, 1992.)

2 Science Workshop: Capturing the Essence of Scientific Inquiry

Jeanne Reardon

In 1991, I began using a workshop approach to support children's science learning. There have been changes outside and within our classroom since then, but the excitement of my first year's Science Workshop has not faded. Each year children arrive with new questions and curiosities that call out for understanding, and so their investigations change; science tradebooks, materials, and resources change; expectations for children's knowledge and understanding of science change. My excitement continues because Science Workshop captures the essence of scientific inquiry. It surrounds teacher and students with the exhilaration that comes from searching for answers to our own questions.

How Does an Inquiry Begin?

I begin this chapter with the story of my own inquiry. It is both an inquiry and an adventure story—filled with the stimulation and tension of exploring the unknown. It is the story of starting a science workshop: Where should the story begin? How does an inquiry begin? In 1992, I wrote the following for this book's first edition (Reardon 1993, 21–22):

> The story begins with a notation in the spiral notebook I keep of my "Curiosities, Questions, and Concerns": "What is so different about how we are learning science and the way we learn reading and writing [—become readers and writers]?" As I played with this question, I thought about the reading and writing community that develops in our classroom each year; I realized we did not have a similar community of scientists. Then came pages of questions. Here are just a few:
>
> What does a scientific community look like? How does it work?
>
> What does a child scientist look like? How does a young child become a scientist? Are there developmental stages most of us go through? Are they the same for the different sciences?
>
> Am I a scientist? How? What do I do that scientists do?

There were also questions about what scientists do:

How does a scientist solve a problem? What are problems to scientists? How does a scientist decide when a solution is *the* solution?

How does a scientist convince other members of the scientific community to accept an idea or explanation? What is convincing to a scientist?

When do scientists set aside an idea/solution/explanation? What makes them set it aside?

What do scientists do when they get stuck? How do they decide what to do next?

Often we think of inquiries as beginning with questions or even hypotheses, but this is a mistake. My inquiry did not really begin with those questions written in my notebook; it began much earlier. My inquiry sprang from numerous classroom observations entered in my journal, from listening to the audiotapes I made of children at work, from replaying children's conversations in my head before I fell asleep or as I drove to school, from reading, and from conversations with colleagues. Watching, listening, writing, reading, talking, replaying, and wondering about what is happening prepared the way for this inquiry. It is the same with our students. Their science inquiry questions derive from their experiences and explorations of their world and books, talking with and listening to friends, from immersion in a topic. Whether adult or child, after considerable observation, we notice things that surprise us; we want to understand what is happening, and we ask questions. We begin to investigate. Later in our inquiry, we wonder, "What would happen if . . .?"; and then we try out different possibilities.

What did I hear in a first-grade classroom that prompted my inquiry? The comments I heard during science time were short, impersonal, and lacking in commitment and detail: "We're studying shadows." "We're watching shadows." "We're drawing shadows." "We're writing about shadows." Occasionally I heard the excited voice of a six-year-old scientist: "I'm watching to see what will happen when I move the light down lower on this box. See, the shadow looks like this when I move it low on the ball, and so on the box . . ."

During reading and writing, these same children overflowed with personal and detailed comments about their work:

I'm reading the last *Curious Dog* book that I wrote, and I'm thinking about what's going to happen in the next one. I'm calling it *The Curious Dog Returns*.

> Jennifer and I are talking about *Little Raccoon and the Thing in the Pond* [Moore 1963]. We're trying to figure out if it's the same Lilian Moore who writes the poems. I think it is, 'cause she writes like a poet. Listen . . .

> I'm stuck in my writing, so I'm reading for a while. That's what you do. It helps you and it helps me.

> Mike's asking me some jokes he's making up for his joke book and I'm listening and guessing the answer. Want to try?

> I'm writing a letter to my cousin in India. She sews so I'm telling her about the square I made for our Harriet Tubman quilt.

I'm reading . . . thinking . . . talking . . . figuring out . . . stuck . . . asking . . . listening . . . —this kind of talk is familiar to teachers whose children engage in writing workshop and literature discussion groups. Any one of the children might have added, "That's what readers and writers do." The children saw themselves as readers and writers who engage in the same activities, share the same concerns, struggle with the same problems, and come to understandings in the same way as those in the larger literate community. We, the children and I, knew each other as writers and readers and sought ideas, responses, and help from others in our writing/reading community. Science was different. Few children had a personal stake in their work; basically, we studied and repeated what was already known in science. We did not know each other as scientists and there was little need to ask for ideas, responses, or help from classmates. We were not a community and we were not scientists.

My classroom observations led me to ask, "What is so different about how we learn science and the way we learn reading and writing— become readers and writers?" Personal experiences as a reader and writer, and experience using a workshop approach in teaching reading and writing helped me think about the impact of our writing community. I wondered if our community contributed to the differences in the way the children talk and function during writing/reading and during science.

I held strong beliefs about conditions essential for students to become writers: Student writers need time to think, to explore possibilities, to try out their ideas, and to write without interruption. They do what all writers do—they write, think, revise, talk, publish. Students write for real audiences, from their own experiences, concerns, and interests. Their teachers trust that they will grow as writers, that they will question, analyze, and discover without continuous teacher intervention. All writers in the classroom, students and teacher, are members of a community of writers who provide support, response, critique, and audience. I continued to think about how our writing/reading community developed and how it worked. I continued to reread my journal writings and to write about my thoughts and questions. It was only then that I wrote the many questions in my "Curiosities, Questions, and Concerns" notebook—for example, What does a scientific community look like? How does it work? What does a child scientist look like?

That summer I participated in the Elementary Science Integration Project (ESIP) institute. The group was made up of kindergarten through grade eight teachers, half with particular interest and expertise in reading/ language arts and half with science interest and expertise. Here was an opportunity to watch and listen to elementary science teachers as, together, we investigated, read, wrote, and discussed. I hoped to begin answering a few of my questions, to come up with some possibilities to try out in September. I was looking for something to fill in the blank spaces in some of my questions: "What would happen if we_____during science?" "How would doing_____build a community of scientists?"

I was still mulling over my problems when Anne Schmidt, a teacher in Baltimore and a Lucy Calkins (1986, 1994) disciple, said: "I think I'll try a science workshop in my classroom." Aha, I thought, maybe it is the workshop structure that helps to hold our writing/reading community together. Maybe a workshop in which we do what scientists do will help build a scientific community, one that will change how we engage in science learning.

Getting Started—A Belly-Smacker

In the fall I moved to a new school, Brooke Grove Elementary. It is a suburban school north of Washington, DC, and a change from the Title I schools where I had taught in the past. The community was new to me; I knew none of the children or parents. I wondered if I should wait and establish myself before beginning something so new, but decided to go ahead with a science workshop.

Two of the children came to our first-grade classroom able to read a little, and one was familiar with writing workshop from his kindergarten. Soon we were all doing what emerging writers and readers do—struggling to make meaning, sharing words and illustrations—often delighted, sometimes frustrated. By the end of September, our version of reading and writing workshop had taken over the morning and it was time to take the plunge into science workshop. I share that plunge as it happened. (The quotations are unchanged. I have not polished my words, though I was sometimes tempted.) It was indeed a plunge, not an Olympic dive cutting through the water without a ripple. It was more what we called *belly-smackers* when I was a kid. They stung, but the water in the lake felt great.

"What do you think will happen when we have science workshop this afternoon?" I asked the class as we gathered together that Monday morning to go over the plans. "Take a few minutes to think and write down your ideas." I wondered if I were prepared for what would happen next. I began writing. I paused and peeked to see how the children were doing. Most were just sitting (I hoped they were thinking), a few were writing and drawing—after all we had only been in school a few weeks. I wrote some more. "Well, what are you thinking?"

The children began, "It'll be fun." "We'll get to decide what we're going to do." Several children passed—that's an option in our discussions. "We'll make potions" (giggles and 'yeah's). "Will you read to us?" "We'll talk." More passes. "We'll write and draw." "We'll make experiments." Finally Matt said, "I don't know what scientists really do, and I don't know what I'll do."

It was then that it dawned on me that I didn't know what we were going to do either. Although I had taught science for twenty years, had taken science courses in college, and regularly read science articles in the newspaper, I had not really thought hard about science as a discipline. But I continued:

> We'll be finding out about scientists and what they do. And one way we'll find out what scientists do is by being scientists ourselves. We're finding out about writers by writing, talking about how we write, reading what other writers have written, and thinking about how their writing works. Science Workshop will be a little different because . . . because . . . the stuff of science is not words and books. It's . . . other stuff. We just look around and see and read what writers have done. We go to the library or bookstore and get it, but we don't go to the science store, pick out what other scientists have done, and figure out how it works for us. . . . Just like we get to write in writing workshop, we'll get to . . . to . . . "science"—We'll just have to make up new words for what we do. I know some things scientists do and that's where we'll begin this afternoon, but I don't know very much about scientists. It's something I plan to find out.

Since that Monday morning in late September, I have thought, written, and talked about what that "stuff" of science is. Just as formerly wherever I looked I saw the work of writers, now I see, think, and wonder about science and technology wherever I look. As Tatiana sharpens her pencil, Seth dilutes the paint, or Karessa cranks open the window, as the dried mud cracks where the puddle had been on Friday . . . I see science and ask the questions of science. For me, now, the stuff of science includes the accumulation of knowledge built on the investigations of many scientists; the new connections I make to old understandings. Science, for me, is the patterns recognized and unrecognized. It is sometimes found in books, in drawings, in symbols, and in writing. It is found in the questions asked; the questions pursued; the explanations proffered, accepted, or rejected.

It is what scientists and children do when we provide them with the opportunity.

Afternoon came and we had our first Science Workshop. We met together in a circle on the rug as I explained how we would work:

> For the first few Science Workshops we'll begin with a minilesson about something scientists do when they are doing science. Then we'll all do some science using materials and tools of science. We'll have problems to solve just like real scientists, and we'll have a scientists' meeting, like real scientists do. We'll get to write about what we're doing.
>
> Today's minilesson is about observing—observing the same way as scientists. Scientists observe in a way so that they can describe *how* they observed and *what* they observed. The *how* is very important to a scientist because some other scientist will want to observe exactly the same way.
>
> First, I'll try out some observing with you. I'm going to use this rocking chair. I could look at it and tell you what I see from where I'm sitting. That's important to say because it may look quite different from where you sit. Let's try that . . . Now I could also observe *what happens when* I do this. [I pushed down on the tip of one rocker as I spoke.] Another scientist would want to know more than "I pushed the rocking chair." She'd want to know that I pushed the rocker down with my hand until the very tip touched the rug, then I let it go, and it rocked and it rocked and it rocked slow-er and sl-ow-er until . . . That's what I mean by a scientist's way of observing. It's more than the what I saw or heard or felt or smelled—it's the how also.
>
> On the circle table, you will find some things [four tubs of pattern blocks—flat, wooden blocks of different geometric shapes, each shape a different color—and two tubs of Tinker Toys™], things I thought you might want to use to build with while you observe. I bet you can build lots of different things. I will say "Stop" every now and then. That means everyone stops and observes. Then we'll share our observations.
>
> One other thing—in writing workshop the tables are quiet and the writing talk goes on at the edges of the room. During science workshop, this will be reversed; the tables will be for science talk and science work; if you want to work without interruption, you'll need to move to the edges. When I call your name, pick up some building material and get started. Remember to think about how you are observing.

That is how we began. I had put a great deal of thought into selecting this first minilesson. I wanted it to be real science. I wanted it to be about something critical to science, and I chose observation. I wanted this first minilesson to engage the children in an activity that would produce varying accounts so that I could better teach the importance of observation. (I would soon discover that every activity resulted in varying accounts.)

I am embarrassed to say that my first thought had been to plan a science *exercise*. I considered setting out five different materials and having the children observe and describe them. Then the part of me that knows kids and writing said, "Why should they observe that stuff? There is no need for them to look closely at that. It's just your need for them to do it." It was then I thought about using construction materials. It was still *my* plan. I knew what I was going to teach. Fortunately, the kids saved me from myself. They began building. As I looked around at their growing constructions, I picked up a small block and began to wonder: "What was I doing?" I was about to build their science out of small blocks, one piece at a time. We didn't write and read by having me pass out one word at a time, and I realized that we couldn't build our community of scientists that way either.

I moved in to watch their construction. I saw boys with all of the Tinker Toys™, girls with the pattern blocks, boys building up and girls building flat. One of the girls went over to get some Tinker Toys™ and was told, "You don't know how to use these." The maleness and the exclusionary nature of science came flooding back to me. My journal from that day contains comments and questions:

> How did it happen that you had to already be good at science, to have proof and the right answers, before you were allowed into the club? Where did the authority of science come from: "Don't come in unless you have all of the facts, and you can't get the facts unless you are in." Six years old and already . . . What's going on here? It's no wonder so little science learning goes on in classrooms—so few elementary teachers ever were admitted to the club. Is it something inherent in science—cold, hard, objectivity without emotion. Is that what science is really like . . . ?
> It's going to be different in our room. We're really going to build a community—and it's going to include the girls!

Now, with ten years of science watching behind me, I would stay with the students' buildings, discuss the gender issue, attend to their science, and extend it. We would become engineering scientists. But this was September and I was still taking belly-smackers. I watched that first afternoon, handled the gender comments, then gave the class a new observation problem the next day. (You take a belly-smacker because you're afraid to go in headfirst, so the last moment you pull your head up, and then—smack.)

Going in Headfirst

It was a hot October day, we had just returned from PE, and I had begun reading *Frederick* by Leo Lionni (1967) when we were startled by rain pounding against the windows. I thought for a moment it was hail; it certainly was a sound that demanded our attention. I suggested we move to the windows to find out what was happening. We looked. The children were riveted to the windows; as we all watched the rain I thought, "This is it. This is the catalyst to set off a real scientific exploration. Sound, light, color, reflections, weather, drops . . . . What shall we focus on? What are the students ready for? What can they do now? Where is their interest?"

I remembered Bernie Zubrowski, an author and scientist from the Boston Museum of Science, who had worked with our Elementary Science Integration Project over the summer. Bernie had said certain materials are intrinsically interesting. Water fit! I saw myself as a child standing by a window watching and wondering: "Which drop will let go first? When those two bump, what will happen? Which will win the race to the bottom?" Drops are interesting, they move, they're easy to make, and watch, and manipulate—they change. Later, I discovered that girls come into science on the same footing as boys when the material is water. I said to the class, "Look at the glass; don't look through it."

After watching another five minutes, we met back on the rug to talk about what we had noticed. "Big drops go faster." "No, some big drops don't go at all." "Little drops go fast when they hit a trail—then they zoom right on down." "I didn't see that." "Let's go back and look." So we went back to observe some more, but the rain was gone as quickly as it had come: "The drops are disappearing!" We met again on the rug. I knew the problem we would work on for our next Science Workshop. I asked, "How can we study and find out more about those raindrops inside our classroom? What if a scientist wanted to find out more about raindrops falling on the window; would she have to wait until the next rain? Be thinking about this for tomorrow's workshop."

Our next workshop began with a quick write in response to our problem: "How can we find out more about raindrops inside our room?" Some children wrote, others drew experimental designs. Everyone had an idea as we worked on a problem common to other scientists—how to replicate natural phenomena in a laboratory setting. Valita even wondered if the drops would be the same when we brought them inside. We talked about laboratory study and field study. I wondered with the kids if studying living organisms changes them. We dealt with safety concerns when we talked about using glass. This moved us into a discussion of materials we would use in our room. An hour had passed, and we were still on the rug working out our plans.

You might be surprised that a verbal science exploration could hold six-year-olds' attention for that amount of time. I think it is an indication that we were exploring a problem that was important to us. Similarly, I found that children would remain engaged in discussion for thirty to forty minutes during our Scientists' Meetings.

As I look back, this was the day we began to build a community of scientists. We had a real problem that we needed to solve before we could go on. It was ours, unique in the sense that no one had ever met and solved this exact problem before. Others have investigated drops of water, but no one had brought the problem into our classroom. It was up to us to figure out how to bring those drops in and to find out how they worked. I am not suggesting that it is never appropriate to read what others have done, to see how they may have approached your problem. But I believe that if emerging scientists are going to experience science in a way that will lead them to understand the processes of science, we also need to give them opportunities to look to themselves and their classmates as problem solvers and science authorities.

We decided that we would need a substitute for glass, and noted that we had plenty of water at the sink. The kids would bring in materials that water could run off of or drop on. Making the drops would be our problem for the next workshop. I brought in several pieces of Plexiglas®, and set out a stack of Styrofoam™ lunch trays, newspapers, and plastic cups for water. (Our school lunches are served on Styrofoam trays similar to those used at grocery stores. The used trays are sent out for recycling but are also available for classroom use.) I also made wooden sticks and drinking straws available as alternatives to fingers for "drop" making.

Before the next workshop I explored drops myself using these materials. I did some thinking about:

- Organization of materials and setup and cleanup procedures
- Students' writing and recordkeeping (logs, paper, format, time for writing, possible prompts)
- My own recordkeeping (audiotapes, notes, status-of-the-class forms)
- Scientists' Meeting arrangements (where, when, procedures, recordkeeping for the meeting)
- Possible minilessons

This became the list I used regularly as I went over what had happened during a day's workshop and prepared for the next workshop. Some of the items became routine: organization of materials, cleanup procedures, my recordkeeping on self-stick notes, status-of-the-class notes. We always included a Scientists' Meeting in our workshops, though the purpose and structure varied from day to day.

The next afternoon's plans read: "After music we'll have Science Workshop—we'll explore making water drops." The class had me insert "YEAH!" after "Science Workshop." They could hardly wait. We started with a short minilesson covering procedures for getting materials, then the exploration began. I stopped by the tables, watched, and chatted:

"How's it going?. . . What are you doing? . . . What's happening? . . .What do you notice?" After fifteen minutes, I had the children stop, passed out Scientist's Notebooks (blank journals), and asked the students to write about what they had done, then, "Continue exploring." Most of the children lay on the floor and wrote for about fifteen minutes then went back to the tables. After ten minutes more, I had the class stop to clean up, and then bring their Scientist's Notebooks and a pencil up to the rug for a Scientists' Meeting.

The Scientists' Meeting

I knew that if the students were going to develop critical-thinking skills in science, they would need to have a forum for discussion. I had thought about ways scientists share their work, questions, problems, and findings and decided that an informal meeting of scientists would be appropriate for first grade. I introduced our first Scientists' Meeting by saying:

> One way scientists find out what other scientists are working on and thinking about is by reading. Scientists write a lot so there's lots to read. They write for themselves, for magazines, and for journals; they write reports and letters. Of course, they talk to each other too. Another way they find out is by going to meetings. Sometimes the meetings are small with just a few scientists who are working on the same kinds of things; sometimes there are big meetings of scientists from many countries. One or two scientists report their work to a group and the rest listen, ask questions, talk, and argue about the ideas they hear.
>
> Usually we'll have one or two of the scientists in our room discuss their work, but today we'll talk around the circle and I'll be the recorder. First, I want you to think about something you *did*, or something you *observed* or noticed, or something you *wonder about*. You'll want to read what you wrote in your journal to help you remember. After you decide what it is that you want to share, write a "D" if it is something you *did*, an "O" if it's something you *observed* or noticed, and a "W" if it's something you *wonder* about. Then, put your journal and pencil down and get ready to listen to the other scientists. (For more about coding notebook entries, see Chapter 5)

When we share all around the circle, it is important for each initial contribution to be short and focused. This technique of coding and marking a response helps the children pick out one thing to tell. The following list brought us partway around the circle:

- "I used my fingers to make drops and the water hung on and wouldn't let go."

- "I made puddles."
- "I cut my drop in two with the Popsicle® stick."
- "You can pull water around with a stick. It just follows the stick."
- "I can pick up water with a straw and let it go in big drops."
- "Some drops are taller than others."
- "Drops fall cause they're heavy."
- "I had drop races."
- "You can blow drops all around and make them bump into other drops until they get so big they aren't drops."
- "Drops jiggle."
- "Drops are hard to see. It'd be easier if we colored them."
- "I put foil on my tray and they went faster."
- "When I put a stick in my cup it looks sort of broke. I took it out and it's not. I put it back and it's broke again."
- "Just before drops fall they change shape."

I recorded everything, writing the child's initials by the contribution, then read over the list of observations, activities, questions, suggestions, and explanations. You notice that not all of the students' comments fit my categories of observations, procedures, curiosities.

Some children regularly give explanations or cause-and-effect relationships while observing—"Drops fall because they're heavy" "Water follows the stick." I came to see these as responses to unspoken questions. Later in the year we worked to take apart a premature explanation and to uncover the question that lay behind it. Once we had the question, we could investigate, collect and analyze data, and afterward offer explanations.

Next I directed the children to draw a line across their pages to mark the end of their original entries, and below the line to write anything they wanted to try for themselves, find out more about, or to talk over with someone. If they were interested in the comments of another student, I suggested they write the name of the child who had done the work so that they could get together. Then I had each child tell me his or her plan for the next workshop. In Writing Workshop I record plans at the end of a workshop on my status-of-the-class sheet (Atwell 1987, 1998). I find that it helps first graders to make plans at the end of each session. During the next Writing Workshop, I read this list for confirmation. I might ask, "Michael, you're continuing with your joke book, right?" We followed this same practice in Science Workshop.

Meetings Help Science Workshops Evolve

During the first few weeks of Science Workshop, I maintained the structure that serves us so well in Writing Workshop. In writing we begin with a minilesson and then spend most of our time writing, conferring with peers and/or teacher, revising, editing, and proofreading. We conclude the workshop with authors sharing their completed pieces (or writing-in-progress) along with discussion and celebration.

In Science Workshop, we also began with a minilesson, followed by hands-on work and writing, and concluded with a Scientists' Meeting. Minilessons were short and focused. Scientists' Meetings gave the student scientists an opportunity to report their work, communicate their explanations, question and challenge each other. Although the structure worked for writing workshop, I found it was not quite satisfactory for science workshop. During meetings we were often confronted with a variety of observations, findings, and explanations. Sometimes these were contradictory. It was not always easy for the children to support or revise explanations, and yet this public forum never seemed like the right place for me to pursue contradictions and misunderstandings. I worked with individual children and small groups to develop their conceptual understandings during the hands-on portion of the lesson, but again, this interaction was not wholly satisfying. More time was needed to focus on students' scientific knowledge, to read informative trade books, and to guide the students to a deeper understanding of concepts and the ways of science.

I had observed that in our Scientists' Meetings the children were very accepting of each other's findings, but at the same time they wanted to try things out and see for themselves. After we began using water colored with food coloring to make our drops, color became an important factor in observations and explanations—"Red drops go faster than yellow ones." "I split my green drop and got little blue drops out of it." Other children, or I, would ask more about such observations so that we could try the same thing. The need for demonstrations became apparent, so we began to schedule demonstrations as part of Scientists' Meeting. This provided an opportunity for on-the-spot questioning and clarification. At this time I introduced replicability as an important scientific practice. While the ability to replicate became important to many children, there was still widespread belief in, and acceptance of, the one-time occurrence. (This observation led me to another inquiry concerning what counted as evidence, what was persuasive or convincing to children of this age.)

The student demonstrations pushed our understandings forward but were not enough. Next I experimented with replacing our minilesson with an, as needed, longer class meeting at the beginning of Science Workshop. These meetings focused on a misunderstanding or problem, something I had noticed or overheard during hands-on work time or a scientists' meeting. During this time, I might read from a book and think aloud with the class or pose a problem in both a general and a specific form:

> Today we are going to think about explanations. What kind of evidence will account for or explain what we observe? What convinces us that an explanation really explains what is happening? Yesterday Mike reported he could push water right through wood. He said that he had two Popsicle sticks and when he pushed down on the top stick, he was able to push water all the way through the bottom one. Mike told us how he knew—the evidence he had. Remind us how you knew, Mike.
>
> "I felt under the bottom stick and it was wet and I'd been pushing down on it."
>
> I want you to write down, or draw pictures of a test you could use to convince yourself that Mike's explanation, pushing down, really explains the water under the stick. Then we'll share our tests and try them out.

Designing fair tests was difficult for these first-grade students, and it never got much easier for some of them. Most of the children considered another class member's explanation to be evidence. They saw no need for tests. "There's a hole in the stick, that's how the water gets there," became a test. Valita was the first, and one of the few that year, to isolate and control variables when designing tests. "First you have to make sure your hands are dry, and the sticks are dry, and the table you set it on is dry. Then you put the top stick in water and press it down hard on the other stick. You get someone else with dry hands to feel if the water went through."

I do not teach lessons on variables to first-grade children, but let the idea emerge or develop from the need to communicate with and to convince others. Afterward I explain that this is one of the ways scientists work; it is a convention of science work just as punctuation is a convention of writing. (Scientific communication is different from the ways of poetry. We expect poets to think and write in metaphors, but would be uncomfortable if a scientist told us, "The rain, they say, is a mouse gray horse that is shod in a silver shoe . . ." [Bennet 1937].)

I find, however, that second-grade students demonstrate great interest in variables. It is part of their obsession with fairness—"That's not fair!" is a frequent reaction to situations in science where control of variables is missing. After an introduction to the new terminology second-graders' responses often change from "That's not fair!" to "That's not fair—you didn't control the variables!" The relationship between evidence and explanation, however, continues to be shaky for many second-grade students. I find that it is not until third grade that children consistently use evidence in constructing their explanations.

Changes Observed in the Students

The first year of Science Workshop provided opportunities for students to engage in activities, share concerns, struggle with problems, and come to understandings in ways similar to those of practicing scientists. The first change I noticed was in the excitement and involvement of the students. No longer did I hear the short, impersonal comments. "We're studying . . ." was replaced by excited voices telling each other about their work:

- I'm pulling water around with this Popsicle stick and I think the stick is like a magnet for water, and then I looked in the hand lens at the stick and it's got little hooks, so now I think it's like Velcro®, and I'm trying to figure out which it is. Do you think it's like a magnet or Velcro?" [Question posed to a fellow student.]

- I'm watching and looking for changes when I put the water here— it's got oil on it, and this—it's got wax. See the water spreads out here, and . . .

- I'm thinking about water, how you can cook it and make steam, and then get the water back . . . That doesn't work for eggs.

- I was reading what I wrote in my Scientist's Notebook and I've got all these strange things so next I'm going to go back and try . . .

These student comments demonstrate more than excitement and involvement. They are an indication that these children have internalized some of the behaviors of inquiry—asking questions, looking for answers to questions, observing change, building explanations based on observation, making connections between what they already know and new observations, planning investigations to understand "strange" things.

Our Scientists' Meetings provided opportunities for students to both describe and demonstrate their investigations. Their descriptions became more detailed as their fellow scientists demanded more information. Students took responsibility for planning what they would do next, often influenced by the explorations and investigations of their classmates. A few children considered alternative paths of investigation, but most were content to investigate one path then move to more exploration. Students asked more questions of themselves and of their classmates, but most questions addressed to classmates remained at a basic level: "What did you do?" or "How did you do that?" Children posed many "How does it work?" and "What's going on?" questions to themselves as they explored, but these questions did not often transfer to follow-up investigations. Rarely did this group of investigators produce cause-and-effect questions and explanations that got at the underlying conceptual and theoretical understandings of science.

Exploration and Investigation

I distinguish between exploration and investigation. In our classroom, exploration and investigation are not limited to science but are carried on across the disciplines. The materials, questions, and data collected differ, but the process is the same. Exploration is an engaged wandering and wondering through materials and ideas; it is a getting-to-know-the-possibilities time and a questioning time. The student explorer is free to select from material to explore and the manner of exploration. (As a teacher, I may limit the materials or provide a focus for the exploration to guide students' attention toward particular content, form, function, problems, and so on.)

Exploration brings with it responsibilities. Students must be able to discuss what they did, what they noticed, and what they are thinking about. This means having a written record to refer to during the follow-up discussion time. The record is usually an entry in a student's exploration log, or perhaps notes on bookmarks or sticky notes, or drawings. Explorations enlarge the child's reservoir of information and experiences. The exploration discussions open the child to alternative ways of seeing and describing and to other ways of interpreting and explaining. Open, wide-ranging explorations and the follow-up discussions are generative. They promote flexibility and result in connections and questions, problems, and possibilities to pursue. Exploration is essential to questioning.

Investigations are focused pursuits in response to a question, curiosity, or problem. They have rules and standards for evidence. Student investigators expect to be asked, "How do you know?" The student audience expects to be shown evidence. An investigation requires a different kind of recordkeeping—a scientific drawing, observations and careful descriptions of "What I did and what I noticed." Investigations may include surveys or interviews. They provide students with a process to use when gathering and analyzing data to answer specific questions, solve problems, and build explanations. Investigations also provide an opportunity for discussion that questions and challenges procedures, evidence, and explanations. I doubt that investigation is possible without exploration, but it is quite possible to explore and never move on to investigate. This is the reason I make the distinction.

Clarification and Answers to Questions

Specific suggestions are useful and I have embedded practical procedures within this account of my inquiry. However, as a conference presenter and inservice instructor, I know that readers are still looking for clarification and answers to their questions. This section contains responses to questions that I am asked frequently. My comments apply to a wide range of classrooms in kindergarten through grade five elementary schools.

Tell me more about the time schedule for Science Workshop. Typically Science Workshop begins with a class meeting of ten to fifteen minutes. During this time the teacher provides instruction in the form of a mini-lesson that focuses on developing a skill he anticipates the students will need in the day's investigations, or a previously taught skill that needs revisiting and refinement. (Sometimes a longer lesson is substituted for the minilesson; in this case, thirty to forty minutes will be needed.) At the end of the meeting the teacher quickly reads down the class list recalling each student's plan for the investigation period. (Students may have planned additional observations, data analysis, exploration, consultation regarding findings, planning a presentation to the Scientists' Meeting, and so forth.)

Next is a period of thirty-five to forty-five minutes when students work independently or in small groups on their own inquiries. Students make entries in their Scientist's Notebooks, recording observations, questions, data, and so forth, as they explore and investigate. (See Chapter 5 for a description of the Scientist's Notebook.) During this time, the teacher focuses and supports inquiries by listening, questioning, suggesting resources; he challenges students to look for alternative explanations; he assesses progress, identifies needs, and selects skills to teach during minilessons. During the last ten minutes of this inquiry period, students write in their notebooks. This is not a summary of what they did, but their reflections and/or comments about the day's work. Finally, they record their plans for the next workshop.

At the conclusion of the inquiry/exploration/investigation period students come together again for a Scientists' Meeting (thirty to forty minutes). This meeting provides time for students to present their work and try out their ideas before the community of scientists (classmates) to receive feedback and respond to their questions. Students may:

- Present data from their inquiry in progress and request ideas for data analysis.

- Present a report of findings and generalizations or explanations from their investigation.

- Demonstrate a procedure they are using or a fair test they have devised.

- Present a problem they are struggling with and request help or ideas from others.

The teacher facilitates discussion, encourages participation, and records students' questions on a chart. She may have the class write a further reflection to a prompt she has chosen. (See Chapter 5 for a discussion of prompts.) At the end of the Scientists' Meeting, she records each student's plans for the next workshop. You will quickly develop your own abbreviated form for recording student plans.

Science Workshop requires a minimum of ninety minutes. A two-hour block of time is ideal. Students need to know that they will be having Science Workshop two or three days every week. When they know the scheduled days for inquiry, they think through their plans and play with possibilities in their head in anticipation of the workshop. Often, the follow-up questions are ones like these:

- How do you teach the required curriculum?

- Do you have two different times to teach science—one for workshop and another for required science?

- How do the students get the basic knowledge they need?

I am tempted to say that all of the required curriculum can be taught as well as learned during Science Workshop. Most primary-grade science units can be strengthened by using school-supplied curriculum materials within a science workshop, because the expectations for student learning outlined in most primary science curricula are minimal and easily reached using a workshop approach. I realize that in some states the science curriculum requires a great deal of science knowledge but with little understanding of science. Often, there are specific vocabulary words and facts to be learned, most of which can be remembered more easily when taught as part of meaningful inquiry in a science workshop.

The upper-elementary science curriculum may be more problematic, especially if the required content knowledge does not lend itself to hands-on classroom inquiry. When secondary sources of scientific knowledge are used rather than student investigations, the teacher's role as an inquiring reader is crucial. The teacher must think aloud about the scientific knowledge presented in textbooks, computer databases, and news articles, questioning the authority and accuracy of sources.

In reality, science and the science curriculum is learned not only during science time, but throughout the day. I read aloud, and think aloud, with the class every day and many of my selections are science trade books. (Chapter 4 provides an in-depth presentation of science reading.) I often use books to deepen students' understanding of the required science curriculum. Children frequently read science books during their self-directed reading time and check out other science books to read at home; I make sure that curriculum-oriented books are always available. The writing done by students as part of reading/language arts units supports and sharpens their scientific writing. (More about writing in Chapter 5.) Measurement skills are part of art and music as well as mathematics and science. Physical education class provides many examples of physics concepts.

Could you give us a list of minilessons to use?   As you watch and listen to students, you will notice common needs. If only one or two students need a particular kind of assistance, you can encourage another student to help. Minilessons are for anticipated or observed common needs. Keep them short, ten minutes, and focused—only one thing at a time. Whenever possible, I use student work, with the student's permission, as the content of the minilesson.

Here are a few minilessons that I have used with younger children:

- Setting out rules for safety
- Letting the class know where materials are kept
- Telling them how to get help from other students, books, Internet, teachers, and so forth
- Cleaning up
- Signing up for demonstrations
- Modeling Scientist's Notebook writing
- Coding entries in Scientist's Notebook
- Showing how to use tools (hand lens, balance, timer, and so forth)
- Demonstrating how to read diagrams and charts
- Making scientific drawings, labels, charts, and so forth
- Organizing data
- Planning what to do next
- Working on a specific problem (e.g., How can I tell what the worms are doing if they live in the ground where it's dark?)
- Modeling different kinds of records to keep
- Discussing lives, work, concerns . . . of scientists relevant to the current area of study

With increasing age and experience students' investigations, explanations, and inquiry skills become more sophisticated. As students mature, minilessons change to meet new needs. Some minilessons I have used with older students have focused on:

- Describing procedures so that others can replicate your work
- Learning how to use various measurement tools
- Reinforcing safety precautions

- Evaluating evidence
- Using evidence to revise an explanation
- Looking for alternative explanations
- Designing fair tests
- Looking for patterns and analyzing data
- Reviewing the various ways scientists record observations and data
- Showing students ways to display findings

What if students don't have any questions to investigate? The younger the students, the more easily they generate questions—excellent questions. The difficulty is that young children's questions may not be testable within the classroom or within their abilities. With first- and second-grade children, I often need to say:

> That's a really good question—"How do little cells know to turn into bark or roots?" Scientists have been wondering and working on that question and are still working on it. Most of the scientists working on your question have specialized tools to help them in their investigations. There are some questions and problems that are too difficult for us to solve in our classroom.

I am fortunate to live in the Washington, DC, area and am sometimes able to get a scientist with the specialized knowledge, and the ability to communicate with young children, to come visit with the class.

Unfortunately, the longer students have been exposed to textbook science and follow the directions experiments, the more difficult it is for them to pose authentic questions. Students in upper-elementary grades need lots of time for exploration. It helps if the teacher models authentic questions by wondering aloud as she stops by tables during exploration. The more exploration I do myself, the more questions I have. It is now difficult for me to observe students exploring and not think of questions. I have to tell myself to keep quiet.

How do you teach the skills of science—things like classification and data analysis? Many skills are taught during minilessons, or the extended lessons at the beginning of workshops. I also take advantage of situations during exploration and investigation time. When I observe a student demonstrating a skill, or a unique way of solving a problem, I call out, "Stop for a minute and come over here." The class gathers around the student who talks with the class about what he is doing. I find that skills and techniques are best learned when they are being used, demonstrated, and explained by a fellow student.

Opportunities for pattern recognition and data analysis can be found throughout the day. One of my most successful data analysis lessons came in response to a first-grade child's question, "How do you know if a word begins with 'c' or with 'k'?" The data had already been collected for us in a variety of dictionaries. All the children, regardless of their reading abilities, were able to study the collection of words and participate in the analysis. "There's way more 'c' words," one commented. "How can we be sure," I asked. After I started a chart, the children counted words in different dictionaries and did the recording. "There's hardly any 'ka' words in my dictionary." "Mine either." "I've got a big dictionary and it's got 'em, but they got capital 'K' at the start." The analysis, counting, and recording continued. The index in the atlas confirmed many proper names beginning with "K." For the remainder of the year, data analysis in science was associated with the *c/k* experience in spelling.

I introduce ideas, skills, and practices of science before all of the children are ready. I agree that there is developmental appropriateness and readiness, and children only assimilate what they are ready for. I also find, however, that one way children become ready is by hearing ideas introduced and seeing them practiced by their peers. Sometimes this is as simple as acknowledging and naming scientific practices as I observe them. Perhaps I point out Nancy Winslow Parker's use of symbols in *Frogs, Toads, Lizards and Salamanders* (1990) or remark on how a classmate has put his drawing inside a hand lens to show it is magnified. Sometimes a skill used in science is more easily absorbed in another context.

If I use Science Workshop will my students pass the state-mandated tests? If the tests reflect the *National Science Education Standards* (NRC 1996), then your students will do very well. The *Standards* call for

> more than "science as process," in which students learn such skills as observing, inferring, and experimenting. Inquiry is central to science learning. When engaging in inquiry, students describe objects and events, ask questions, construct explanations, test those explanations against current scientific knowledge, and communicate their ideas to others. They identify their assumptions, use critical and logical thinking, and consider alternative explanations. In this way, students actively develop their understanding of science by combining scientific knowledge with reasoning and thinking skills. (2)

Science Workshop promotes inquiry and understanding of scientific knowledge as described in these standards. Unfortunately, however, not all tests mandated by states assess students abilities as described. If the state tests only assess factual knowledge and neglect the skills and abilities outlined in the *Standards,* we must actively lobby for a change in the tests. It is not easy to find time to take on such a project, but if we do not, students may be denied the ability to do critical thinking, which is such an important part of inquiry into the world about them.

Reflections

My goal in writing this chapter is to demonstrate the potential of science workshop for developing children's scientific inquiry abilities and building their science knowledge. Scientists follow many paths in their inquiries and frequently back up, collect more data, and try a different path. Inquiry is not as neat and efficient as the teacher- or textbook-designed lessons that follow a straight path to teach students accepted scientific concepts and explanations. The abilities central to scientific inquiry develop over time. Over the past ten years, I have noted that, as the Science Workshop takes hold, students arrive at and defend their own explanations based on evidence obtained from the analysis of their data. They more critically evaluate the explanations they encounter in their life outside of school. Students may even grow to question, rethink, and overturn currently accepted scientific explanations.

I hope that by sharing my initial experiences with Science Workshop I have given the reader a sense of the interplay between my personal observations, inquiries, and the evolving structure of Science Workshop. We must be inquirers ourselves in order to model inquiry for students. We must model the curiosity, openness to new ideas and data, and the skepticism characteristic of science. Science Workshop is not a method with foolproof steps to learn and follow. We are often provided with guides to follow: "Steps to Successful Lessons in" . . . reading, mathematics, science, even critical thinking. Such guides are presented with authority and simplicity. I am skeptical of these guides and their step-by-step directions for teaching. Perhaps the steps are the distillation of a complex learning process, but it is important for me as a teacher to hear not only the conclusions reached, but the classroom life behind the learning and the evidence that supports the conclusions. Without the background of alternatives considered and decisions made, I am less able to solve problems when they arise.

Early in this chapter I wrote that when I began thinking about Science Workshop, I held strong beliefs about conditions I considered essential for students to become writers. Ten years later I believe that similar conditions are essential if children are to develop as scientists and critical consumers of science. Science Workshop provides these essential conditions: time, opportunities for students to pursue their own interests in the same way as practicing scientists, and trusting teachers who model the attitudes and behaviors of science. Our students must have opportunities to study authentic problems that arise from their own experiences, concerns, and interests and to develop or select investigations, materials, and procedures to follow. They need time to think, explore possibilities, try out their ideas and work without interruption; to do what practicing scientists do—observe, use tools, construct, measure, plan, experiment, question, gather data, organize data, explain, revise, build theory, argue, test, meet, write, read . . . Their teachers must trust them to grow into scientists and critical consumers of science; it is important to me that they develop the attitudes of science without being directed to the way. For a workshop to succeed, there must be a community of scientists—students and teacher who provide support, response, critique, and audience.

References

Atwell, N. 1987. *In the Middle: Writing, Reading, and Learning with Adolescents.* Portsmouth, NH: Boynton/Cook.

———. 1998. *In the Middle: New Understanding About Writing, Reading and Learning.* Portsmouth, NH: Boynton/Cook.

Bennett, R. B. 1937. "Rain." In *Under the Tent of the Sky*, comp. by J. W. Brewton. New York: Macmillan.

Calkins, L. M. 1986. *The Art of Teaching Writing.* Portsmouth, N.H: Heinemann.

———. 1994. *The Art of Teaching Writing, Second Edition.* Portsmouth, NH: Heinemann.

Lionni, L. 1967. *Frederick.* New York: Pantheon.

Moore, L. 1963. *Little Raccoon and the Thing in the Pond.* New York: McGraw Hill.

National Research Council (NRC). 1996. *National Science Education Standards,* Washington, DC: National Academy Press.

Parker, N. W. 1990. *Frogs, Toads, Lizards and Salamanders.* New York: Greenwillow.

Reardon, J. 1993. "Developing a Community of Scientists." In *Science Workshop: A Whole Language Approach*, W. Saul, J. Reardon, A. Schmidt, C. Pearce, D. Blackwood, M. Bird, 19–38.

3 Inquiry: A Classroom Model

Charles Pearce

It was the first day of school. With it came the anticipation of a new start, and the somber realization that summer was really over. As the students arrived in their new fifth-grade classroom, they were instructed to gather six white beads from a bowl and string them onto a short length of yarn.

"A small welcome back gift," I told them as they tied the ends of the yarn to secure the beads.

"Gee, thanks Mr. Pearce," they politely responded, no doubt wondering how six beads could be a gift.

The school day began and the beads were forgotten—until midmorning.

"Mr. Pearce," Joe yelled with his hand waving. "Look at my beads. If you click them back and forth like this, they change colors."

Sure enough, Joe's beads had changed from white to orange, purple, and pink as he flipped his wrist back and forth, clicking his beads. Other students quickly took out their beads and began clicking them. All around Joe, beads were being transformed from white to a rainbow of colors. The children congratulated Joe for his amazing discovery and realized the beads were a pretty cool gift after all . . . except for the kids on the other side of the room.

"Mine don't work," said one student who was clicking her beads as hard as she could.

"Mine don't work, either," complained another student next to her.

"I'm sorry," I said and told them that maybe I could find some replacements later.

It wasn't until recess after lunch that the truth about the beads was discovered. These were no ordinary beads, and they certainly did not change colors as a result of being shaken. Outside, the children made some interesting discoveries. In their closed hands, the beads were white, but when exposed to sunlight they changed to different colors. Their experiments with shaking and not shaking in the sun and in the shade indicated that movement had no effect on the beads. It was the sun, the kids discovered, that made the beads change.

"Or maybe its heat," others began to ask. Questions and theories and experiments were flowing as recess came to an end on that first day of school.

Joe's original theory, accepted earlier as he demonstrated his discovery at his desk by the window, was no longer viewed as valid now that more data had been gathered. Together, we saw a part of science, experienced countless times through history, as observations leading to discoveries and theories were later updated and revised with the gathering of more data. The children were already beginning to follow this same path as young scientists. My role as their teacher was to clear the way.

First-day ventures into inquiry science are wonderful ways to start the year and set the tone for the science thinking that is to come. Science instruction, it seems, falls anywhere along a scale from highly controlled teacher-centered instruction at one end to student-centered inquiry at the other. Depending on the objectives for lessons being taught and our own predilections, we find ourselves at various points along this continuum. Moving toward the student-centered side can sometimes seem risky. Yet, those teachers who have relinquished a degree of control report a renewed interest and motivation among students. The importance of student ownership of experiences was underscored for me many summers ago during a workshop for teachers.

Reflecting on those experiences and feelings from that summer workshop, I really wanted to enable my students to take a more active role in the classroom. I wanted them to experience the same exhilaration I had felt that afternoon when I abandoned the activity cards and created my own questions and found my own answers. But approaching inquiry-based instruction forced me to consider numerous procedural questions, including the following:

- How could I help my students develop their own testable questions?

- How could I foster active participation for *all* students?

- How could I keep up with the demands of inquiry-based science materials?

- How could I (and my students) be accountable for our time?

- How could I integrate science with writing and reading?

- How could I assess progress?

- How could my *I*'s become *we*'s so that all of us in the classroom might collaborate with one another?

I was part of a group of three teachers at the workshop who were instructed to spend an hour with a box of materials. As the hour began, we eagerly removed the items from the box: a jug of water, salt, several balls, a scale, clay, measuring devices, and a packet of activity cards. Our mission was to follow the directions on the cards and experience hands-on science as if we were the students.

By the time the hour had nearly passed, we realized that we had not even started the assigned activities on the cards. They had been forgotten as we first tried our own activities and then designed ways to answer our own questions. Reporting back to the larger group, we apologetically indicated that somehow we had been sidetracked, seduced by the many possibilities posed by the materials, and had not completed the assigned activities. We had, however, enjoyed our time together and had made many interesting discoveries.

What if, I thought while driving home that day, I tried giving third- or fourth- or fifth-grade students boxes of materials with no directions; no packets of activity cards? There would be no hidden agendas and no regimented steps to follow. Would learning take place? Could that learning be assessed? Would this approach encourage high-level thinking and enable the students to monitor and evaluate thinking processes? Could the curriculum still be addressed if students were afforded a wide range of choices?

A more philosophical question also occurred to me, based on my own recognition that young children are scientists. Preschoolers, playing in the sandbox, are driven by their need to find out. They want to explore their environment, discover how sand can cover objects or be molded into shapes. Their memories recall past play and enable further developments. Play for children is true science at work. Yet, at school, a child's expertise as a scientist is often discounted. Even hands-on science programs provide narrow structures, confining the budding scientist and discouraging divergence. My goal was to foster questioning and thinking; my own questions about science learning were sparking my thinking about science instruction.

Questions and Science

Science discovery is driven by questions. What we do is a response to the questions we are considering. Of primary importance is question ownership. Where do the questions originate? Who really cares?

It is natural for kids to ask questions. My goal has been to help my students realize that they can ask and answer their own questions—often by collaborating with their peers. I began by modeling. Each day I think aloud, asking questions of myself and my students:

- Will oil spilled in the ocean float? How do we know? Can we test this in the classroom?
- Are rocks all the same? How can differences be measured?
- If acorns are seeds, will they sprout and grow?

To many of the questions I have no perfectly correct answers. I might speculate or formulate theories (theories that might later be tested), but my goal at this stage is to help the students feel comfortable with their own questions. We soon discover that a good question often serves as a catalyst for many others. We posted a sign in our room to affirm our confidence: "The best questions are our own questions."

The Question Board

Questioning is the heart of inquiry science. Questions often arise for which a class has neither an immediate answer nor the time to investigate. Yet those questions must not be lost. In our class we began recording questions on the *question board.*

Early in the year we post a large piece of laminated oak tag on which students are invited to write whatever questions they wish. Although part of the magic might be in using the overhead markers, the students seem drawn to the question board for other reasons as well. This is a place where they can publicly share their questions and read the questions of other students. Figure 3–1 shows a portion of a question board.

Students write questions before and after class, or during class discussions when a question arises for which no one has an answer. By having the question board available early in the year, we can examine the process of questioning and look at types of questions.

Within science there are basically two types of questions: research questions and testable questions. *Research* questions can be answered by *re*searching what someone else has already done and can be answered best by reading a book or using the Internet. *Testable* questions, on the other hand, are questions that the students themselves might answer by doing something. Either through observations or experimental design, the students themselves discover the answers to their own questions.

As the question board is filled, a committee of students copies the questions for publication. The printed questions are then used to discuss the differences between research and testable questions. Although questions such as "How hot is the center of the sun?" may not appear to be

Figure 3–1.   A fifth-grade question board.

testable, one student pointed out that with the proper tools nearly *every* question about the physical universe is testable. By using the question board, students can examine their own questions and distinguish those that can be readily tested from those that cannot. Later, we use these experiences to design our own experiments.

Thinking Scientifically

Putting students in control of their own learning enhances motivation. Kids who make choices or design activities are kids who think about learning. This process internalizes values and provides ownership for the learner.

My work in teaching thinking was premised on two assumptions. First, I realized that activities that were not teacher-directed would require far more thought. Activities for which students had to tap their prior knowledge and to create their own questions entailed more thought than those that required only answers or the completion of blanks on a worksheet. Second, I assumed that *all* students could think at these levels, especially if provided with opportunities to do so. To engage students in authentic scientific thinking, the problems and questions under consideration had to emanate from the students themselves.

Activities traditionally thought of as language arts based, when applied to science instruction, proved helpful. In activities, such as *Know–Wonder–Learn* (Donna Ogle 1986), students first list three or more facts they know about a topic, then write three or more questions they have. Later, after reading a passage or doing an activity, three or more things students learned are listed. This activity links prior knowledge with new knowledge. I understood that without tapping prior knowledge, inquiry science would be like a bottle set adrift, hollow and disconnected. The K–W–L model has more recently become a *Know–Wonder– Learn—and Wonder Some More* spiral. We have found that new knowledge prods even more questions, and the students have come to realize that with each answered question come many more questions to explore.

Reciprocal teaching (Palincsar and Brown 1986, Coley and DePinto 1989) was another strategy utilized. Students in small groups had been discussing and summarizing what was already known, questioning one another, identifying and clarifying what might be confusing if younger students were present, and predicting outcomes or what might happen next. These think tanks were great for language classes and proved effective in science as well.

As the students gained confidence in questioning and problem solving, they were no longer merely recipients of facts and directions, and I was no longer the only decision maker in the room. Our roles began to change. As the year progresses, science instruction moves across that continuum from a more teacher-centered approach near the start of the year toward a far more student-centered environment. I have come to value this transition because of the student progress it yields.

Inquiry science, however, is more than asking questions and thinking like a scientist; rather it is a spiral of questioning, thinking, testing, recording, and questioning again. The teacher's role is to provide a workable framework for all of this activity. In our classroom, that framework has been provided by the discovery boxes.

The Boxes

Discovery boxes have become an important component of inquiry science in our classroom and were developed as a direct result of my experiences at the Elementary Science Integration Project summer workshop. These moderate-sized plastic tubs contain related items on a particular theme. In conjunction with the use of the question board, the discovery boxes have been a natural extension for real-life, hands-on inquiry. Once children feel comfortable developing testable questions, the boxes serve as a resource to help investigate those questions.

Each discovery box contains a number of items to aid students as they design experiments. Trade books on the theme of the box concept provide background and often spark new questions. Materials useful in testing, safe for independent use, and related to the theme are found in each box. An essential component of each discovery box is a folder in which students record information (see Figure 3–2 for an example of a completed discovery log page). The folder reinforces the concept that with the freedom of investigation and discovery comes the responsibility of documentation. The records in the folders serve not only as a means of accountability, but also as a way for students to communicate with one another as scientific colleagues.

Finding topics for discovery boxes was not difficult. Some of the topics arose from questions on the question board; others were related to our science curriculum. However, interesting topics need not be limited to the current grade level of the students. One day Brian asked, "What would happen if I hooked up five batteries to one flashlight bulb?" He was putting his knowledge from the previous year's science class in which he had studied electricity to use.

It is natural for kids to want to carry on with ideas from previous years, but far too often they are not afforded the opportunity to do so. Children's interests and questions do not turn on and off with the end of a unit or a grade. There is no reason why kids hooked on magnets in third grade should not continue to explore magnetism in grades four and five. Creating boats and experimenting with sinking and floating can be as compelling a topic for older children as it is for those in kindergarten. Topics we investigate in our class each year include magnets, electricity, liquids, mealworms, soils, light and color, boat building, and rocks and minerals.

SCIENCE DISCOVERY LOG

Activity _Boat Building_   Names _Phillip_   _Meredith_

Date _01/21/1_   _Aubrey_

What question did you try to answer?
What is the highest buoyancy ratio we can make?

Explain what you did to answer your question.
We made a boat that could hold
more than its weight. We used
straws and a sponge to make
a boat, weighed it, and then put
a weight on it. The ratio was
1.2E.

Make a sketch of your experiment.

straws
weight - 55.58g
sponge
4358g - boat weight

What did you discover today?
We discovered that a boat can hold more than its weight.

What new question are you curious about for another time?
Is it possible to make a boat with a higher buoyancy ratio than ours?

Are you pleased with your results today?   YES ✓   NO ___   NOT SURE ___

How would your group rate this activity?   Great 10   9   (8)   7   6   5   4   3   2   1   0   Terrible

Figure 3–2.   A completed page from the Boat Building Discovery Log. The sketch of the boat is a rough drawing. Entries in the Book of Discoveries require a much clearer representation for future replication.

Included in the liquids box, for example, are a variety of measuring instruments and containers, and supplies such as water and vinegar, food coloring, pH paper, sugar, salt, filter paper, soil, and more. Also included are possible questions for students to attempt to answer, although they are encouraged to investigate their own questions. With tubs and buckets, and a sink if one is available, the children can immediately begin manipulating the materials.

The mealworm box contains straws, pipe cleaners, string, colored construction paper, and, of course, mealworms. These creatures can be obtained inexpensively from most pet shops and are the perfect animal for classroom investigations. Students enjoy them by observing how the mealworms react to edges and obstructions, seeing which colors they appear to prefer, or noting changes as the colony ages.

Included with the discovery boxes are backup boxes. In the spiral of questioning and investigating, kids develop many ideas. It is sometimes difficult to predict which questions will be pursued or what additional materials may be needed. I try to have on hand what the students might need when a hot topic is being investigated. Thus I have several resource boxes to supplement the materials in the discovery boxes. The resource boxes contain materials, such as aluminum foil, pipe cleaners, flexible straws, clay, toothpicks, construction paper, salt, paper cups, and wooden sticks, that might be useful. There are neither directions nor suggestions, simply possibilities. The students always find interesting ways to use whatever is provided.

How and When

Time is the most challenging aspect of inquiry-based science. When in the day can kids go off and explore their own interests? And in a class of twenty-five or thirty students, how can this be organized? After a bit of experimentation, the students and I developed the *inquiry* period.

An inquiry period, which might occur several times a month, is a fifty-minute time block in which groups of two or three students work together with discovery boxes of their own choosing. A day or two in advance, students sign up for and reserve a particular discovery box (see Figure 3–3). Before the inquiry period, the children are given time to look through the boxes to examine the materials and determine if anything else might be needed for their own investigation. (See Figure 3–4 for an example of the form used to prepare for the inquiry period.) Also available before the inquiry period are the trade books found in each box. These books are wonderful tools for providing additional knowledge on a given topic and are also useful in inspiring new questions. However, the most important preinquiry-time activity is having the students read the entries in the discovery logs in each box. In these logs, previous students have recorded their questions and investigations. By reading the log

CHOICES FOR:
TUESDAY, DEC. 10

A. LIQUIDS BOX   Dawn C   Paige   Kristina

B. ELECTRICITY BOX   Kevin W.   Brooks S   _____

C. MEALWORMS BOX   Julie C.   Tiffany D   _____

D. SOILS BOX   Corey S.   _____   _____

E. ROCKS & MINERALS BOX   Jennifer L   Lindsay H.   _____

F. MAGNETISM BOX   Ginger T.   Sarah R.   _____

G. HOURGLASS WORKSHOP Jamie L   Jenny Bindon _____

H. TOWER WORKSHOP   Anton   Jacob   _____

I. FILMSTRIP WORKSHOP Bridgett S.   Jeff Miller Charis T.

J. MEDIA CENTER   Jamie S.   Lisa R.   _____

K. _____   _____   _____   _____

L. _____   _____   _____   _____

M. _____   _____   _____   _____

N. _____   _____   _____   _____

O. _____   _____   _____   _____

P. _____   _____   _____   _____

Q. _____   _____   _____   _____

R. _____   _____   _____   _____

Figure 3–3.   A sign-up list for an inquiry period.

Plan for Inquiry Period

Name _____ Date _____

Next Inquiry Period _____

Day and Date _____

BOX, TOPIC, or CONTRACT to be used: _____

(If CONTRACT, list contract name and number) _____

Testable Question you will be trying to answer: _____

_____

_____

Materials to be used: _____

_____

_____

_____

Are the needed materials available in the classroom now?   YES   NO

If "NO," which materials are needed?_____

_____

_____

_____

List any special needs necessary for your investigation. _____

_____

SUBMIT THIS FORM TO YOUR TEACHER AT
LEAST 24 HOURS PRIOR TO INQUIRY PERIOD.

Figure 3–4.   A planning sheet for an inquiry period.

pages, the students not only see what others have done but may also think of additional questions or find an experiment that they wish to replicate. Later, students add their own new entries to the logs.

A few ground rules have proven helpful. First, students are expected to stay with their selected activities. It is best to avoid having children jump from one thing to another, losing their focus and disturbing others. For those who finish early, observing what others are doing or quietly reading is acceptable. However, students know that they are accountable for their time. In addition to the discovery log sheets, journal entries, or other written documentation, I often distribute What I Accomplished . . . forms (Figure 3–5) at the end of the period. These forms enable students to summarize what they have done and help me assess how they used their time.

The inquiry period gives me the opportunity to visit with small groups of students as they embark on their own investigations. By asking questions or engaging in dialogue, I am able to participate in the activities with the children. The time I spend with each small group enables me to give more personal attention and provides valuable feedback for assessment.

When the inquiry period is over and the classroom is finally clean, we have our debriefing. This class discussion is critical in the development of our scientific community. Each group shares with the class the box that was used, questions investigated, and discoveries made. For many, this is an exciting time to publicly proclaim the amazing things that were accomplished in the small group. This also helps to advertise each box so that when the next sign-up occurs students may be attracted to a topic that might not otherwise select. Additional details about inquiry periods, discovery boxes, and inquiry period debriefings can be found in *Nurturing Inquiry* (Pearce 1999; see also "Thinking Science" video).

The Science and Writing Connection

One exciting result of the popularity of the discovery boxes has been the enhancement of communication skills used to record and share student discoveries. Scientific writing by the students has taken many forms. Recording data on the log sheets in the discovery boxes is just the beginning; students also write in dialogue journals, the class Book of Student Discoveries, and in writing workshop. The children write for different audiences and for different purposes.

Just as journals have been used in language arts to share and comment on student ideas about books, activities, and events to remember, journals are also used for scientific thinking on paper. Journal entries include discussions of ideas and experiments performed with materials in

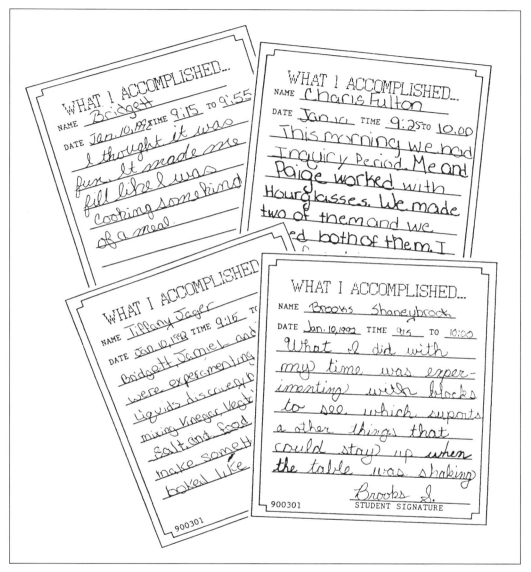

Figure 3–5.   Several examples of completed What I Accomplished . . . forms.

discovery boxes, as well as thoughts and questions for further exploration. Moreover, journal entries allow the students to communicate with me on paper and afford me a place to record responses. For scientists, an important feature of journal writing is its permanence. Both the students and I are able to return to read previous entries again and again.

In addition to records made in the discovery logs and journals, students can also document discoveries on a Scientific Discovery Sheet (Figure 3–6). The Book of Student Discoveries binder, which resides in our class library, provides each student opportunities to publish results of investigations for others to read. Entries stay in the book even after the school year has ended, which means that students can read about discoveries from previous years. Plus, as students contribute to the book they know that students next year or in the years to come will be able to read what is written.

Prospective entries must progress through a series of steps before final acceptance. Student peer review is an essential part of this process. Our Science Review Board (SRB) is a committee of three students who examine each entry. Their job is not to replicate the investigations (that is left for later students), but rather to check for the inclusion of sufficient details so that later replication will be possible. With a wide degree of latitude, the SRB also determines if the discoveries appear to be reasonable. Should the Review Board not accept an entry for inclusion in the book, a written explanation must be made to the contributor explaining why the entry was rejected and suggesting what might be added before resubmitting. Usually, however, the SRB accepts and signs the entry and sends it along to the Spelling Police—a committee of two students who are charged with ensuring that all published work in our classroom contains no spelling errors. Finally, the document arrives at my desk with the proper initials and dates, and I am able to announce another entry for our book to the class.

The Book of Student Discoveries is another source of authentic reading in our classroom. Some students may be inspired by what others have written. In attempting to replicate experiments, students must follow the procedures written by others. It is apparent that clear writing is essential and this realization helps motivate students to improve their own writing. Student authors of entries in the book will not be present next year to explain their ideas. Their writing must say it all. Figure 3–7 shows the back of the page on which future students record the results of any replications that may be attempted.

Inquiry science experiences have also served as prewriting activities for writing workshop. As investigative stories unfold, students have found interesting topics for their writing. The growth of crystals, observations of mealworm colonies, planting of seeds, or soil conversation on model mountains are just a few of the writing topics that have come from scientific investigations. Since these investigations were not teacher-assigned, student ownership enhances the motivation to write. The relative quiet and reflective nature of writing workshop time enables the children to think in depth about their science experiences. Science process and content have been intriguing fodder for the workshop.

Scientific Discovery

971031

This discovery was made by *Leana Byrne*
STUDENT SCIENTIST(S)
on *Feb. 27, 2002* .
DATE

DISCOVERY: *I discovered that when a mealworm first turns into a beetle it's white, then it turns brown, after that it turns black.*

The following steps were taken which led to this discovery.
(PLEASE INCLUDE SPECIFIC DETAILS WHICH INCLUDE MEASUREMENTS, QUANTITIES, AND
ONE OR MORE SKETCHES OR DIAGRAMS.)

1. Sign a contract for mealworms. And get the mealworms.

2. Wait till it turns into a pupa.

3. Then wait till it hatches into an adult, (beetle)

4. A few days later it will turn brown, then black.

| White | Brown | Black |

SKETCH

Confidence of Accuracy (circle one)
HIGH LEVEL OF CONFIDENCE 10 9 8 7 6 5 4 3 2 1 0 LOW LEVEL OF CONFIDENCE

Figure 3–6.   A sample Scientific Discovery page from a Book of Student Discoveries.

Replications

I. *The experiment/observation described on the front side was repeated by*

_____
student scientist(s)

on _____.
date

Results: _____

_____

☐   ☐   ☐
Results Similar   Results   Results
To Original   Inconclusive   Different from
Discovery   Original Discovery

- -

II. *The experiment/observation described on the front side was repeated by*

_____
student scientist(s)

on _____.
date

Results: _____

_____

☐   ☐   ☐
Results Similar   Results   Results
To Original   Inconclusive   Different from
Discovery   Original Discovery

- -

III. *The experiment/observation described on the front side was repeated by*

_____
student scientist(s)

on _____.
date

Results: _____

_____

☐   ☐   ☐
Results Similar   Results   Results
To Original   Inconclusive   Different from
Discovery   Original Discovery

Figure 3–7.   Experiment replication sheet.
© 1999 by Charles R. Pearce from *Nurturing Inquiry*. Portsmouth, NH: Heinemann.

Science, Technology, and Kids: The link between science and technology was portrayed in an entertaining way by James Burke in his PBS *Connections* series. Weaving his way through history, Burke shows how each seemingly minor scientific discovery is linked to the next in a progression that has led to many of our present technological marvels. Science is portrayed as being useful. Recreating authentic experiences in the classroom has been one goal of the inquiry approach. If we can make our own discoveries technologically useful, we can provide purpose for our inquiry.

One day Adam came to school quite excited about some rocks he had found in the forest behind his house. "I think they are calcite," he said as we carefully examined each one.

"How do you know?" I asked.

"Well, they look like those calcite rocks from when we worked with rocks and minerals."

"Yes, they do," I agreed, "But how can we tell for sure?"

"We could use vinegar to see if they fizz," Adam suggested.

I was a bit surprised. Adam was a student who was a challenge to motivate, yet he had apparently remembered what we had done several months earlier as we explored mineral testing and identification. Adam put a few pieces of his rocks into a small plastic cup and poured vinegar over them so that they were submerged. Sure enough, the rocks began to bubble. Everyone was impressed with Adam's success.

"Maybe," Adam said, "I could make a discovery box with my calcite and vinegar and other things for kids to work with. They could try doing other things, too." I liked Adam's idea and suggested he begin work during our next inquiry period. But the story was just beginning. Like one of those mistakes or accidents that led to scientific discoveries in the past, Adam's plastic cup was set aside and forgotten. The following Monday morning Adam discovered that the vinegar had evaporated and a white material was covering the calcite.

"That must be chalk," he announced.

"Why do you say that?" someone asked.

"Well, isn't chalk calcium carbonate?" he asked.

"Is it?" I asked, surprised again with Adam's knowledge.

"Yes, it is," some others answered.

"Calcite is, too," Adam said. "This white stuff must be chalk!" With that, he took a piece of the white material and wrote his name

continued

on the board. Even though it crumbled in his hand, Adam had indeed used the material as chalk.

Then Adam made that technological link. He planned to go back to his forest, mine more calcite, crush it, mix it with vinegar, wait for the vinegar to evaporate, and make chalk to sell to the teachers in our school. He would implement his plan from raw materials to a processed product and then market his product for profit. Based on a database of prior knowledge, Adam was making his own connections on his technological journey.

Adam formed a small group of students to assist with his chalk *company*. He lost interest in the discovery box idea (which was okay), and his chalk company had some serious manufacturing problems, but the process was unfolding in a way that Adam would never forget.

Scientific inquiry for Adam and his group continued as they struggled with possible binding agents to keep their chalk from crumbling. Their experiments yielded other products. One chalk "failure" yielded a by-product much like concrete. Adam never found the manufacturing secrets of chalk production, but his experiences led the class to new levels of scientific thinking. His adventures were among others that led off of the curricular path and onto parallel byways of learning.

The Science and Reading Connection

A clear link between inquiry science and reading has been noticed in our classroom. The use of discovery boxes has encouraged independent reading of a variety of trade books. Although the books found in the boxes are seldom used during the excitement of an inquiry period, the books have been read with interest when a part of each day is set aside for quiet, independent reading. We use DEAR (Drop Everything and Read) time for students to read materials of their own choosing. Often, children select books from a box they plan to investigate during a future inquiry period or from a box they have used recently. Students also take advantage of DEAR time to read from the Book of Student Discoveries. They enjoy seeing what others have discovered and find that reading others' work enhances the development of their own questions.

Student inquiry in the classroom has also influenced book selection at the library. By investigating their own questions, students are motivated to seek books that might help answer specific questions or that might give clues toward solving a particular problem. From their authentic experiences, students are motivated to think about topics, find books based on their interests, and then use what they have read to shape further inquiry. This process of learning is the way adults learn—not by fulfilling someone else's assignments, but by engaging in experiences that truly interest and can yield more questions and journeys into inquiry.

Beyond the Boxes

It would be a mistake to consider the discovery boxes *the* destination. There is far more to inquiry science than boxes of materials. The spiral of student questions and investigations with the eventual discoveries and dissemination lead to even more questions asked by the students. It is this inquiry cycle (see Figure 3–8) that builds on itself and makes teaching science so exciting.

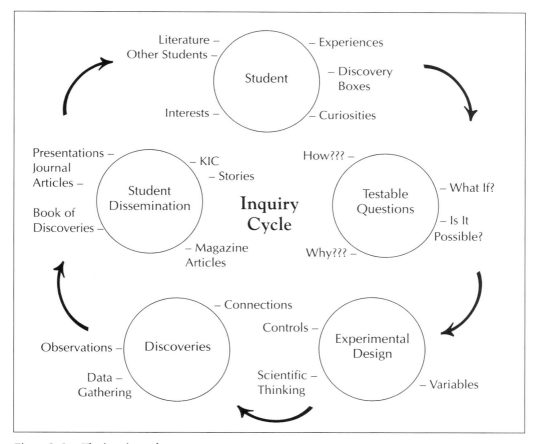

Figure 3–8. The inquiry cycle.
© 1999 by Charles R. Pearce from *Nurturing Inquiry*. Portsmouth, NH: Heinemann.

There was a time when I believed that the ultimate in science instruction was the hands-on revolution of the 1980s. It was with *hands-on* that the materials, once reserved for the teacher's lab table, were placed in the hands of the children. With carefully planned directions and specially selected materials, hands-on science offered step-by-step procedures to lead students through an array of activities. Yet, this cookbook approach to science has been highly teacher- and curriculum-centered. The traditional hands-on approach with its preconceived outcomes is quite different from authentic science and the ways in which children do science on their own.

Young children, whether at the beach, in the playpen, in the backyard, or in the park, constantly explore and manipulate their environments. Through their play, children gather an amazing amount of data in response to problems (towers of blocks that will not remain standing) or questions ("What happens if I pour water into a hole in the sand?"). Children in this sense are scientists! They are driven to find out. In their play, children follow few directions from others.

I remember watching, for what seemed like hours, my daughter Emily playing at the seashore. She had dug a hole in the sand and was filling it with water. The hole was a fair distance from the surf, so she had to carry her bucket down to the water, fill it, and carry it sloshing back to the hole. With each trip her task seemed to become more and more of a hopeless cause. Even though the sand was wet, the water was always gone. Her persistence interested me. What kept her going? Occasionally she stopped to examine the sand but would soon continue with her work. Several things became apparent to me.

First, it was obvious that Emily was enjoying herself. Just being at the beach, whatever the activity, was special for her. I also began to notice that she was learning a lot. The properties of water and sand—sand's permeability and how water seemed to disappear in it were fascinating to her. For Emily, and countless other children, the beach was her laboratory. But I asked myself. What if I had taken a group of students to the beach and instructed them to dig holes in the sand and then spend hours lugging water from the ocean and pouring it into the holes only to watch the water disappear? I suspected that those students, like most other children, would soon complain that they were tired or hot or too thirsty to continue after a few minutes. Plus, what would be the point? The water would always be gone.

The most important ingredient in Emily's activity at the beach was ownership. It was *her* activity, not mine. The questions she was answering and the problems with which she was dealing were her questions and her problems. Her motivation to persist came from within.

So it is with the children in our classrooms. Sure, they need direct teacher instruction, through hands-on, to learn how to use the materials and to understand the processes of science. Emily was able to use her shovel to dig a hole in the sand because she had learned how from her dad at some earlier time. But the shovel and the bucket did not then disappear. Nor should the materials in our classrooms. Here is the value of the boxes. Those materials don't go away. They are available time and time again to pursue answers to those questions, new or old, or to search for solutions to problems.

But the discovery boxes are *not* the destination, although, like hands-on, at one time I thought they might be. Many of the children grow beyond the boxes as they gradually assume ownership of more complex investigations. Fifty minutes is simply not enough time to adequately handle some of the ongoing investigations that evolve. Here again, time is a critical factor.

One solution has been our use of *inquiry contracts.* A contract provides accountability in an environment of autonomous, divergent activities. Contracts clearly state what is expected from the student—research, documentation, sharing, and so forth—and what the student can expect from the teacher—primarily time—since the students are exempted from certain assignments. The sample Teacher/Student Contract and Inquiry Investigation Plan shown in Figure 3–9a and 3–9b detail these expectations. Contracts can be worked on during inquiry periods or other times of the day. Since some classroom assignments are exempted, students with contracts often do their work while others are completing regular assignments. Typically, contracts last seven to fourteen days for in-depth study. The contract journal consists of several pieces of folded 8-1/2″ by 11″ plain paper with a piece of construction paper folded over as a cover. A more complete description of a variety of contracts and how to use them, as well as inquiry enhancements beyond the discovery boxes, can be found in *Nurturing Inquiry* (Pearce 1999).

The Kids' Inquiry Conference

As the year progresses, student autonomy grows. The children are embarking on their investigations, based on their own questions. Some have teacher/student contracts that provide for the time inquiry investigations require. More questions are appearing on the question board. Entries are being made in journals and on log pages as well as in the Book of Student Discoveries. The children have assumed the roles of authentic scientists—asking questions scientists ask, thinking in ways that scientists think, doing things that scientists do. Our community has grown, and we ask tough questions of one another, not as competitors, but as skeptical thinkers and collaborators. With discoveries to share and stories to tell, the stage is set for the Kids' Inquiry Conference.

While talking with Susan Snyder of the National Science Foundation one summer morning many years ago, an idea began to unfold that led

TEACHER / STUDENT
C O N T R A C T

CONTRACT NUMBER _____
DATE _____

_____ agrees to work on the following long-range assignment:

CONDUCT A SCIENTIFIC INVESTIGATION

to be completed on or before _____

The classroom teacher agrees to provide a reasonable amount of class time by exempting the student from selected classroom assignments.

Completion of this contract (will / might / will not) require additional time at home.

The following provisions apply in the completion of this contract:

*The student will prepare a contract journal.

*The student will attempt to answer the following testable question:

_____

_____

*An *Inquiry Investigation Plan* will be completed (on back of this form).

*Daily entries will be made in the contract journal in which activities, observations, data, sketches, and notes will be recorded.

*The results of the observation will be recorded in the contract journal.

*Discoveries will be recorded in the *Book of Student Discoveries.*

The student agrees to do his / her best work on the completion of this contract.

_____
STUDENT

_____
PARENT

CLASS _____

_____
TEACHER

Figure 3–9a. Teacher/Student Contract for scientific inquiry investigations.
© 2002 by Wendy Saul, et al., from *Science Workshop, Second Edition.* Portsmouth, NH: Heinemann.

Inquiry Investigation Plan

Name _____ Date _____

I am interested in (topic) _____

I would like to attempt to answer the following testable question: _____
_____

I predict that _____
_____

The following materials will be needed for my investigation.

MATERIAL	SOURCE	MATERIAL	SOURCE
_____	_____	_____	_____
_____	_____	_____	_____
_____	_____	_____	_____
_____	_____	_____	_____

To answer my question, I will do the following:

(First) _____
_____
_____

(Next) _____

_____

_____

_____

(Then) _____

_____

_____

_____

Sketch (with labels)

I will need ____ school hours per week, and ____ home hours per week for my investigation. My investigation will take approximately ____ weeks to complete.

Teacher Notes:

Figure 3–9b. The Inquiry Investigation Plan describes details of the student investigation; it is on the back of the Teacher/Student Contract for scientific inquiry investigations.

to an event that now takes place each spring. What if we could hold a conference in which children from different schools would come and present the results of their ongoing investigations to one another? There would be concurrent sessions with break-out rooms, poster sessions, displays, and a keynote speaker. This conference would be like a conference for adults, but with children as the participants. Could this forum work to further student investigations? Would the children be interested in the investigations and discoveries of others? Could a dialogue be started in which child-scientists might actually discuss the merits of their collected data with one another? The idea of a conference for kids was born—the *Kids' Inquiry Conference* (KIC).

From the outset, the goals of this children's scientific conference were ambitious. Our hope was to provide opportunities for students to do the following:

- Share the excitement of their own discoveries

- Interact with students from different schools who have common interests

- View science as a dynamic force in their own lives

- Consider, critically, the credibility of their own research and the research of others

- Draw on the discoveries of other students to enhance their own research

We were fortunate to have the assistance of the Elementary Science Integration Project (ESIP) as we planned the first KIC. The goal was to provide a working model of a children's scientific conference that could be organized without extensive help.

The setting for the first conference was the campus of the University of Maryland, Baltimore County. Not only was that campus a central location for the schools involved, but it led to a more scholarly meeting for the fourth-, fifth-, and sixth-grade students participating. Three classes from three different schools (a total of ninety students) came together for the first KIC.

The conference was divided into three forty-five-minute sessions with various meeting locations for each session. During each session, at each of the locations, three or four students or groups of students shared the results of their investigations and what they hoped to accomplish next. Many of the students attending did not present, but added to the conference by asking questions from the audience. It wasn't long into the first KIC session that we realized we were really on to something wonderful for the kids. They were asking questions of one another, examining each others' data (especially those who were investigating similar topics), taking notes, and behaving as scientists do at conferences. Since that first KIC, conferences have been held at other college campuses, in hotels, and at corporate headquarters.

Each February or March, students who have stories to tell about investigations and discoveries are invited to complete an application to do a presentation at a Kids' Inquiry Conference (see Figure 3–10). Presentations are about eight to ten minutes in length, introduce the question that is being investigated, give some background information on the topic, tell exactly what was done to answer the question and what discoveries were made, and identify additional questions future scientists might want to investigate.

The application process provides an opportunity for students to briefly describe their investigations and to explain what they will do during their presentation to convince the audience of the accuracy of the data. Sometimes each individual classroom teacher reviews the applications and decides who will be presenting. Often, teachers whose classes are attending a KIC meet to review applications together. Knowing that someone other their own classroom teacher will be looking at the applications encourages the students to work even harder to portray their investigation as one worthy of selection. Virtually all students applying are accepted to present at the conference. (Those whose applications were not accepted are encouraged to reapply and include details or information that was lacking.)

The students complete and send off their applications and await the replies. To heighten the drama, I like to place the responses from the "committee" into an overnight envelope and have it appear at the school office. When our secretary calls to tell us a package has arrived, the kids, who have been expecting it for days, get really excited and nervous. Each response is sealed in its own envelope within the package and envelopes are distributed throughout the class. Screams erupt as the kids read the letters and tell each other they have been accepted. What a great feeling it is to find out that someone you don't even know thinks your research deserves to be scheduled for a scientific conference. The elation is short-lived, however, because the kids soon realize what the acceptances really mean.

Imagine being eight or nine years old and confronting the prospect of speaking before a group of strangers. For most of the children, this is their first time in such a situation. As their teacher, my role becomes that of a coach. I reassure them that they really do have interesting stories to tell and guide them as they prepare their presentations. The acceptance letter congratulates each student and briefly describes what is expected. But, in the classroom during the weeks and months preceding the conference, we go into much more detail about credibility, data presentation, how to address a group, and the fielding of questions following a presentation.

KIC:
Application to Present

The Kids' Inquiry Conference Committee is eager to hear about your scientific research and discoveries. In order to plan the conference, your assistance is needed. Please complete the spaces below.

NAME _____ DATE _____

SCHOOL _____

TEACHER _____ GRADE _____

1. Describe any reports or projects that you have prepared for science class in the past two years.

   _____

   _____

   _____

   _____

2. List any science articles or booklets that you have published in recent years (such as in the class or school magazine or newspaper).

   _____

   _____

   _____

3. List two or three discoveries you have made within the past two years, either at school or elsewhere.

   _____

   _____

   _____

   _____

4. Describe the question you are researching and would like to present at KIC.

   _____

   _____

   _____

   _____

Figure 3–10. A blank Application to Present at the Kids' Inquiry Conference form.
© 1999 by Charles R. Pearce from *Nurturing Inquiry*. Portsmouth, NH: Heinemann.

5. Briefly discuss your investigation. What are you doing to attempt to answer your question?

_____

_____

_____

_____

_____

6. How is your research progressing? How would you evaluate the success of your investigation thus far?

_____

_____

_____

_____

7. What will you include in your presentation to convince your audience that your discoveries are valid?

_____

_____

_____

_____

_____

Please sign below if you are willing to present your findings at the Kids' Inquiry Conference. Your application will be reviewed by the KIC Committee and you will be notified of the committee's decision.

_____

SIGNATURE OF APPLICANT

_____

SIGNATURE OF PARENT

_____

SIGNATURE OF TEACHER

Thank You and Good Luck!

Figure 3–10. *(continued)*
© 1999 by Charles R. Pearce from *Nurturing Inquiry.* Portsmouth, NH: Heinemann.

The array of skills learned and practiced takes the children far beyond what any science curriculum might require.

During the early years of the Kids' Inquiry Conference, the problem of materials and the funds to cover them limited the investigations of some of the students. Individual parents were a big help, but there were times when more was needed, especially as the investigations became more ambitious. After trying several different solutions, using funds from our PTA, the Inquiry Grant Program was developed. I convinced the PTA to set aside an inquiry fund from which the children could apply for grants. The Inquiry Grant Proposal Application shown in Figure 3–11 requires a description of the question under investigation, a list of materials needed, and an explanation of how the investigation is to be conducted and evaluated. Grant recipients are expected to furnish a report to the PTA when the research is done. Grants have been awarded in the range of $10 to $20 for such items as batteries, motors, chemicals (e.g., vinegar, cornstarch), wires, and simple building supplies (e.g., special glues or tapes).

Applications for grants are reviewed by a grant committee, which can take one of several forms. A group of students and teachers might examine the proposals, deciding together on the merits of each proposal. I like to involve the Science Review Board (described on page 52) in this process. Students evaluating requests for funds from other students is an important part of peer review. Plus, encouraging students to apply for their own grants helps them learn that modern science requires more than *doing* science; scientists must also be able to *find funding* for their projects. Convincing others that their research is important enough for funding requires students to think carefully about what they are doing and how they are doing it. Communicating the essence of their research to others is just as important as the research itself.

Following the first conference, the students were frustrated about missing presentations that were going on in other rooms from their own. They wished they could have seen and heard more. To help with this and to preserve a record of each year's conference, a journal has been published each year. Student presenters are asked to write up their presentations for inclusion in the annual *KIC Journal*. Not only is the journal a wonderful souvenir of the day, but it has served as a kind of textbook in our classes in succeeding years. Students this year can read what others did in the past. We examine the articles, decide which are most convincing and why, and come up with new questions to investigate. Assortments of *KIC Journals* are valuable resources in our classroom and are used extensively throughout the year.

The logistics of planning and organizing an inquiry conference have evolved through our experiences with KIC. More details about conducting an inquiry conference are available in Barbara Bourne's chapter, "The

Inquiry Grant Proposal Application

Manchester Elementary PTA

Manchester Elementary students who are engaged in or planning a scientific investigation are invited to apply for financial assistance to further their research. The PTA Inquiry Grant committee is interested in all areas of scientific inquiry. Please describe your investigation by completing the spaces below.

Names of students working together on this project _____

_____

Teacher(s) _____ Grade level ____ Date _____

Describe the testable question that this research will attempt to answer.

_____

_____

_____

_____

BUDGET: List the materials needed, the quantities, approximate costs, and sources.

MATERIALS	QUANTITY	APPROXIMATE COST	SOURCE
_____	_____	_____	_____
_____	_____	_____	_____
_____	_____	_____	_____
_____	_____	_____	_____
_____	_____	_____	_____

TOTAL AMOUNT OF GRANT REQUEST $_____

Describe how your group plans to use the materials to answer the question. (Provide a step-by-step procedure.)

_____

_____

_____

_____

_____

Figure 3–11.   A blank Inquiry Grant Proposal Application form.

Provide a schedule of your project. (Include start date, major milestones, and completion date.)

_____

_____

_____

_____

Describe your plans for evaluating the success of your investigation. (How will you know if you are successful?)

_____

_____

_____

_____

Has your group applied for or received financial support from other sources? If so, please describe.

_____

_____

_____

_____

If this grant request is approved, a written report will be required upon the completion of the project. The report is to describe the testable question, materials used for the investigation, how the investigation was conducted, and results of the investigation.

By signing this grant request, the students agree to the provisions described and indicate that the information contained in this application is accurate.

_____

_____

_____

_____

SIGNATURES OF STUDENT SCIENTISTS

A RESPONSE TO THIS GRANT REQUEST WILL BE PROVIDED WITHIN 2–3 WEEKS.

Figure 3–11.   (continued)
© 1999 by Charles R. Pearce from *Nurturing Inquiry.* Portsmouth, NH: Heinemann.

Kids' Inquiry Conference: Not Just Another Science Fair," in *Beyond the Science Kit* (Saul and Reardon 1996) and in *Nurturing Inquiry* (Pearce 1999). There is now a KIC website [*www.umbc.edu/kic*] which contains all back issues of the *KIC Journals*, sample forms that can be downloaded, photographs, teacher and student resources, and a variety of additional information about inquiry conferences.

Assessment

Assessment is an ongoing, continuous process that begins when we first meet our students and continues until the last day of class. All day, every day, I am looking for evidence of progress; from those casual conversations before school to the formal testing situations that are mandated by our school system. I find myself continually asking what constitutes *progress* in an inquiry environment?

Since inquiry focuses on questions, I first look carefully at the questions on the question board. What kinds of questions are being asked? Who is asking them? I look for student questions in journals and on discovery log pages. I look at the entries in the Book of Student Discoveries. How have the questions progressed toward authentic student investigations in which data were gathered and discoveries made. But as important as questions may be, of far more significance to assessment are the student *behaviors* of inquiry science.

From the start, I know exactly what I hope to see in each student. Clearly defined, observable behaviors that indicate an understanding of the processes of inquiry science make assessment possible. Throughout the year I ask myself questions about each student. The questions represent some of the most important indicators that I use to evaluate their progress and the success of my own role in the classroom. The following are some of the questions:

- Is the student asking testable questions?

- Does the student design fair tests to answer questions?

- Does the student read for additional information about a topic under investigation?

- Does the student record data?

- Is the student engaged in self-directed investigations?

- Is the student able to translate observations into usable data?

- Does the student discuss ongoing investigations with others?

- Does the student make connections between different investigations?

Inquiry Science Indicators Checklist

For _____

This student:	OFTEN	SOMETIMES	SELDOM	NEVER
1. Asks testable questions	_____	_____	_____	_____
2. Designs fair tests to answer questions	_____	_____	_____	_____
3. Gathers data in an organized and logical manner	_____	_____	_____	_____
4. Identifies and seeks additional materials	_____	_____	_____	_____
5. Reads for additional information related to an investigation	_____	_____	_____	_____
6. Exhibits an understanding of variables in an experiment	_____	_____	_____	_____
7. Exhibits understanding and use of a control	_____	_____	_____	_____
8. Translates observations into usable data	_____	_____	_____	_____
9. Discusses ongoing investigations with others	_____	_____	_____	_____
10. Exhibits perseverance, especially on investigations with unexpected results	_____	_____	_____	_____
11. Compares data with others doing similar investigations	_____	_____	_____	_____
12. Records data for future use	_____	_____	_____	_____
13. Asks new questions based upon new data	_____	_____	_____	_____
14. Creates or modifies models	_____	_____	_____	_____
15. Engages in self-directed investigations	_____	_____	_____	_____
16. Makes entries in the *Book of Discoveries*	_____	_____	_____	_____
17. Makes connections between different investigations	_____	_____	_____	_____
18. Expresses interest in replicating the investigations of others	_____	_____	_____	_____

Figure 3–12.   A blank Inquiry Science Indicators Checklist form.

These questions and others have become part of an Inquiry Science Indicators Checklist (Figure 3–12), which provides a place to document behaviors that are crucial to inquiry success.

Assessment also includes the *products* of inquiry. Students must know certain facts about the world around them to ask questions and design experiments. Most science curricula concentrate on those facts and provide a means for testing and assessing knowledge. Inquiry science approaches build on the material *learned* and use that knowledge to *push* the frontier of learning farther. The products of inquiry provide tangible evidence of progress in these areas. Examination of discovery logs and journals, entries in the Book of Student Discoveries, Inquiry Grant Proposal Applications, and Applications to Present at KIC, as well as the articles published in the *KIC Journal,* are all evidence of such progress and indicate the authenticity of the science being experienced. Not only are we able to measure what the students *know,* but we can see what they are able to *do.* These layers of assessment provide numerous opportunities to evaluate students. Effective assessment must provide feedback for the teacher seeking to monitor the classroom environment (*formative* assessment) and also provide data useful for measuring the progress of each individual student (*summative* assessment).

As important as all of these assessment strategies may be, the most significant assessment in science is *credibility.* A scientist must convince others that the data being reported are credible. It is through authentic science in the classroom that young scientists face their toughest challenge: convincing their peers. This challenge is the task of every scientist. When children share the results of their investigations with one another, they want to be believed, whether it be in the classroom during our debriefing after an inquiry period or at the *Kids' Inquiry Conference* standing before a room of strangers. Credibility among peers is the most powerful form of assessment. Knowing that others around you believe and trust what you say is more powerful than any grade from a teacher. Plus, as children assess one another, examining what is believable and why, they come to better assess themselves. It is through realistic self-assessment that children truly grow.

What's Next?

Inquiry has come to be a central part of my classroom, not only because of the success I have seen as a result of its use, but also because of the support and validation inquiry approaches are receiving beyond classroom walls. The *National Science Education Standards* (NRC 1996) has become a blueprint for local school districts in the writing of science curricula. Of the six strands described in the standards, the first among them—Teaching Standard A—emphasizes inquiry: "Inquiry into authentic questions generated from student experiences is the central strategy for teaching science" (p. 31).

Indeed, the importance of inquiry in science classrooms has been underscored by the publication of *Inquiry and the National Science Education Standards* (NRC 2000), which specifically addresses many of the issues raised in this chapter. This companion volume to the original science standards (citation p.71) discusses such topics as classroom assessment and inquiry, and preparing teachers for inquiry-based teaching, and the book includes a section of frequently asked questions (FAQs) about inquiry. The *Standards* are helpful in designing curricula as well as justifying the use of classroom time for inquiry activities and strategies.

Inquiry is an extension of previous science instruction strategies. Hands-on approaches were revolutionary in their early stages, yet are now widely accepted as an effective means of science instruction. Because many science curricula incorporate hands-on, it is essential for educators to see the importance of extending hands-on to include the questions and problems of students and to make inquiry a vital part of the busy school day. The growing tide of inquiry promises exciting possibilities for children.

As I have experienced the evolution of science instruction, I find myself asking what the next step might possibly be. With inquiry in place, only the children can answer that question. I never know from one year to the next which direction our science journey will take. Different students with different questions always pose new sets of challenges. This is the excitement of teaching. The children *will* surprise us if we give them the opportunities to do so.*

References

Coley, J. D., and T. DePinto. 1989. "Merging Reciprocal Teaching with Question Response Cues." *Reading: Issues and Practices* 6: 76–80.

National Research Council (NRC). 1996. *The National Science Education Standards.* Washington, DC: National Academy Press.

———. 2000. *Inquiry and the National Science Education Standards.* Washington, DC: National Academy Press.

Ogle, Donna M. 1986. "K-W-L: A Teaching Model That Develops Active Reading of Expository Text." *The Reading Teacher* 39: 564–70.

* *Note*: Many of the topics discussed in this chapter are addressed in greater detail in *Nurturing Inquiry* (Pearce 1999). Also included there are discussions of additional inquiry enhancements: scientists in the classroom, outdoor education, topics for discovery boxes, models in science, and an in-depth description of assessment possibilities and resources.

Palincsar, A. M., and A. L. Brown. 1986. "Interactive Teaching to Promote Independent Learning from Text." *The Reading Teacher* 39 (8): 771–77.

Pearce, C. R. 1999. *Nurturing Inquiry: Real Science for the Elementary Classroom.* Portsmouth, NH: Heinemann.

———. In *Thinking Science: Work in Progress,* created by Wendy Saul in collaboration with the Elementary Science Integration Project, 1995, videocassette.

Saul, W., and J. Reardon, eds. 1996. *Beyond the Science Kit.* Portsmouth, NH: Heinemann.

4 *Reading as Scientists*

Donna Dieckman

It makes a kind of common sense—that students should be encouraged to combine the doing of science with reading about the subject. From my teacher point of view the most promising connections build from and to science-related trade books. Now, however, the professional conversation taking place seems to be moving away from rather than toward the activity of science and the personal scientific interests of students. For instance, there is a lot of talk about the challenges of comprehending information text. Two issues seem to dominate the discourse: the explicit teaching of text features used in information literature and the use of information literature for explicit content teaching.

Teacher workshops have centered on strategies to help students identify and navigate through information text in order to comprehend needed information. Navigation skills are useful and necessary for conducting quick information searches, but in my class, trade books offer much more than straight information. (If students were only looking for information, the World Wide Web (WWW) might serve their purposes better.) In fact, the answer to a single question brings them back to books again and again—to learn more, to listen to the way a given author tells a science story, to check their own understandings and observations against the understandings and observations an author provides. To further explore how science-related trade books work for students and teachers, I wish to share my own nine-year journey in the classroom.

My first job, straight out of undergraduate school, was in a school district transitioning to a kit-based, hands-on science program. Though happy to see these hands-on materials, my own interest was in figuring out how to supplement the kits with really good science trade books. I knew titles and authors and I was anxious to match or coordinate kit topic and books. Eagerly, I set about planning. Learning centers . . . I would set up science centers . . . that should work. I created a visually appealing backdrop, organized materials for investigations, and selected and displayed trade books related to the unit of study.

When we engaged in class investigations, I would place trade books on tables with materials and student journals and invite students to explore the books as well as the materials. There was a small amount of browsing but mostly students were interested in the *stuff*. I would feature some of the books in read-alouds throughout the unit and remind students that the books were available in the science center during independent reading time. There were a few takers, but mostly students enjoyed looking at the pictures.

What Science Books Bring to the Classroom: Books present different approaches to the same subject. When a teacher uses books to demonstrate the many possible approaches to a scientific subject, children's eyes are opened to the diversity and complexity of science. Since trade books are written in a human voice, and are based on the interest and curiosities of a writer, they invite readers to share in the pleasures the science writer has enjoyed in his or her research and writing. Sometimes the language used to pass on the story of science is so intriguing, so inviting, that students try to write a story like that.

- Books model scientific thinking, attitudes, and procedures.
- Books help students to make connections and ask questions.
- Books that present and explain scientific procedures illustrate the how-to of science: observing, experimenting, hypothesizing, and recording. They assist students as they investigate their own questions and enable students to make authentic scientific meaning.
- Books invite students to witness the world beyond their own environment.
- Science trade books can help us understand that science is more than hands-on activity. They help students recognize the connection between what people do and the world in which we live.
- Books inspire intellectual curiosity and wonder.
- Science trade books promote science as a human activity. Often science books include "science people" as part of the story they tell.
- Science-related books engage reluctant readers.
- Excellent trade books exemplify excellent writing. Narration, description, exposition, even creative writing can be sparked by topics of scientific interest.

I had created an environment in which books and science peacefully coexisted in the classroom. We read good science books and we engaged in hands-on science investigations, but there was little authentic interaction between the two. I was mainly *using* books as content sources—filling in the vocabulary (the three types of rocks, the different kinds of clouds), naming parts (parts of an insect, parts of a flower), and providing explanations of phenomena (how a seed grows, the water cycle). While this information can certainly be part of the curriculum, it could just as easily be gotten from a textbook or an encyclopedia. I began to understand that my students were not devouring science trade books the same way they were devouring fiction because they viewed them as *reference* books to be consulted on a need-to-know basis, and usually only in order to complete an assignment.

Our first real breakthrough came shortly after there was an oil spill in a river nearby. In our classroom conversations, several students raised questions about how oil spills occur and how they are cleaned up. We had been investigating the natural environment throughout the year and the students were very interested in this topic, so we decided, as a class, to investigate oil spills.

Two overarching questions guided our quest—"What did we want to find out? How would we go about finding the answers we sought?" I read the newspaper accounts of the spill to students and they brainstormed questions in their science notebooks. At our Scientists' Meeting we created a large web, mapping out their questions. Questions centered around the composition and nature of oil: "What happens when oil and water mix? How is oil transported? What causes oil spill accidents to occur? How is the oil cleaned up? What effects does the oil have on marine life and the surrounding environment?"

Then we used our web to think about our second focus—resources and procedures for pursuing our questions. Students were eager to "mess around" with oil and water in the classroom but realized that many of our questions required more than just materials—we needed information to support our inquiry. In those days, the WWW was just a rumor that those of us in schools mostly ignored, so we decided that our best resources would be books, newspapers, and experts in the field. A trip to the library provided some excellent books. Relevant titles focused on the *Exxon Valdez* oil spill in Alaska and provided background information on the process of transporting oil. A phone call to the Coast Guard yielded more helpful information and an unexpected partnership in our classroom inquiry. While we were asking the Coast Guard representatives our questions, they had a few questions for us: "What type of oil did we plan to use for our classroom investigation? What materials would we use to attempt a cleanup? How would we evaluate success or failure?" We realized we had a lot of planning and thinking to do and used the next several Science Workshops to do it.

Our classroom scientists were so eager to explore and discuss what had been written about oil spills, the books I had gathered didn't ever make it to the display area but, instead, were "gobbled up." We began looking for information but the more we read, shared, and discussed the books, the more we realized that books offered us much more than facts. The information about the composition of oil, the design of tankers, and so forth was pretty standard, but only answered our most basic and least-challenging questions. Reading *Oil in Troubled Waters* (1983) by Madelyn Klein Anderson introduced us to the logistics of an oil spill clean-up operation and provoked much thought about the waste produced in the cleaning process—a problem we hadn't even considered. *Spill! The Story of the* Exxon Valdez (1991) by Terry Carr focused on the short- and long-term environmental effects of one particular spill and caused us to ponder the difficulties of containing a spill with moving currents and wind. *Oil Spills: Damage, Recovery, and Prevention* (1993) by Laurence Pringle addressed the complexity of matching the right clean-up plan with a particular type of spill and inspired a great deal of thinking about the need to have a variety of materials at our disposal.

As we continued to read, we began to formulate our hands-on exploration. Students formed teams to plan various aspects of our shared investigation. We agreed that we would all initially observe oil in water and then construct our own clean-up plans by observing and evaluating various materials for their effectiveness. As students discussed and wrote out their plans, they would often revisit some of the books we read, to think about possible materials. They had read about containment booms, skimmers, and dispersants, and put much thought into how they could approximate such materials in the classroom. Students also were very conscientious about producing waste, so they attempted to design a clean-up plan that would be efficient, as well as effective. After their investigations, they consulted books to compare their findings with those of the authors.

I must admit that my carefully choreographed science center and book display area changed dramatically during this time. Our center became a working center rather than a display center. Student-produced charts, questions, and diagrams covered the bulletin board, and books and materials were inseparable. Students were reading (1) to gather information, (2) to generate ideas for their explorations, (3) to validate their findings, and (4) to gain multiple perspectives on a complex issue.

Books provided time for them to mull over their ideas and inspired them to think much more thoughtfully about their own explorations. By starting from passionate questions about an event in our *backyard*, we ended up in a place where reading about and doing science were parts of a cohesive whole. So this is how the process works, but what about the books themselves? Does it matter if the information is cogently presented?

If it's gracefully written? What image of science and scientists are students left with? In short, is this book good enough for my students?

In 1996, I was invited to be a member for the National Science Teachers Association–Children's Book Council panel that gives awards for the *Outstanding Science Trade Books* in children's literature. This gave me an opportunity to look much more critically at the depth and breadth of children's science literature and to think more about how books about science might contribute to scientific understanding. Looking at science trade books in this larger context, outside the boundaries of a specific topic focus, afforded me an opportunity to consider the scientific thinking and decision-making processes that are embedded in a text. How could I model this newfound understanding and interact with my students in a way that would teach these important ideas?

In our classroom, we were engaged in an exploration of rocks and minerals. There were numerous questions on our question board about volcanoes, a favorite topic of many students. We had marked a *B* for books next to the volcano questions since these were questions best explored through literature rather than hands-on investigations (the vinegar and baking soda volcano model offered little of intrinsic value for exploring our questions). Wanting something authentic and real for them, I chose *Volcano: The Eruption and Healing of Mount St. Helens* (1986) by Patricia Lauber for a read-aloud. This book would satisfy the volcano enthusiasts in our class and introduce students to Patricia Lauber, an eloquent science author.

As I introduced the text, I also shared with students my own curiosity about the scientific thinking that goes into writing a science book, and I asked them to help me think about these more general processes as we read the book. We stopped periodically to look at how the text was structured and to think about why the author might have structured the text in that way. We talked about what information she chose to include in her book and tried to articulate what questions she was interested in writing about. We discussed what methods she might have used to conduct her research and how she used evidence to support her claims. On balance, the oohing and aahing over the sequence of photographs documenting the eruption was far more enthusiastic than the responses to my questions. I was about to deem this experiment a dismal failure—these were hard questions to think about and were premised on a decidedly different way of looking at text than we had done before; perhaps it was simply too difficult. Suddenly, at the end of the book, Aishah raised her hand and said, "I think the author was really interested in life cycles." I asked her to elaborate.

"The story begins when the volcano wakes up, it erupts, a lot of nature is destroyed, the volcano is quiet again and over time things begin to grow again. Someday it will happen again." Aishah's observation about the book rejuvenated the conversation, and we revisited the book looking for evidence to support Aishah's conjecture. Students were now leaning forward, looking closely, and listening carefully.

Chris suggested we use sticky notes to mark places in the text. When I came to Lauber's words, "One day, a hundred years from now, a new forest will be growing on the north slope of Mount St. Helens. Everything that lived on the slope before May 18, 1980, will be able to live there again" (p. 51), a bevy of hands shot up to mark the passage.

Read-Alouds: Reading good books aloud to students is a tradition and a favorite activity in many classrooms. However, science-related literature, especially nonfiction, is often an untapped resource for book selections. Choosing well-written, engaging science books for read-alouds affords teachers the opportunity to introduce students to science-related literature and to model reading and thinking strategies that promote critical thinking. Read-alouds also invite conversation and questions for further exploration, and every reading experience is unique. Here are some things to think about when preparing for a read-aloud:

- Choose a book or section of a book that lends itself to being read aloud. Does the text flow? Is the topic engaging? Are there opportunities for stopping points to wonder aloud? Does the text inspire questions?

- Gather author background information. Many authors of science-related literature have interesting backgrounds that may inspire students in their own scientific or literary endeavors. Many now have their own websites (see pages 116–118).

- Locate relevant artifacts, illustrations, or other hands-on materials that might support the text.

- Think about the focus for your read-aloud and mark talking points—places in the text where you want to stop and reflect or ask questions—to support that focus. This focus could be science-related, or could be related to the author's craft, text features, or literary moves and decisions.

- Identify any keywords or concepts to discuss in context as you read the text.

- Think about connections to other literature—by author, topic, or genre. Collect related books (see Chapter 7 for a description of *Search It! Science*) for a classroom reading display.

Over the next few weeks, I continued to ask similar questions about the texts we were reading aloud. Students were encouraged to think about the science in a book we were reading, or focus on a particular aspect of the author's craft in a particular text. As we became more comfortable with the process, I wanted students to have the opportunity to think about the science in the books they were reading. I created a prompt for them to respond to: "What questions did the author explore in this book?" As they read a book with a partner, I asked students to jot down the author's questions and to use sticky notes to mark passages in the text that supported their claims. As I circulated around the classroom, Michael remarked, "Mrs. Dieckman, this is like what we do in Science Workshop when we have to use evidence to support our conclusions." I hadn't really thought about it in that way, but Michael was quite correct. I had begun by wanting students to engage more deeply in exploring the science in science books, but in the act of doing so, students were actually engaged in a scientific process. Students were reading like scientists.

I continued to think about ways science trade books could support scientific inquiry. In 1998, one of the books being considered by the awards committee was *Snowflake Bentley* (1998) by Jacqueline Briggs Martin. I was immediately captivated by the story of a Vermont farmer who devoted his life to photographing and studying snowflakes. As was often the case, I decided to try the book out on my students. In preparing for the read-aloud, I thought about the many different ways I could approach the book. Topically, there was an obvious connection to snow and winter, but I wanted something greater from this great book. We were used to the question, "What question did the author explore in this book?" As I thought about the answer vis à vis *Snowflake Bentley*, it occurred to me that the question behind this book was really "What is a scientist?" It suddenly occurred to me that while we focused on topics and scientific thinking in books, we really didn't think a lot about how books tell us about the lives of scientists and the work they do.

To activate prior knowledge and elicit preconceived notions about scientists, I began the read-aloud by introducing the question, "What is a scientist?" Students shared reflections about what a scientist does and what she or he looks like. We talked about the characteristics of people that they thought would make good scientists. Then I introduced the book and told students we were going to read about a rather unique man. I asked students to think about the focus question—"What is a scientist"—as we read the story.

Students made comments and asked questions about things they noticed, and I asked questions and thought aloud about things I noticed. We commented that Bentley made careful observations, generated questions based on his curiosities and explorations, recorded accurate and detailed data and drawings of his experiments, used tools of science such

Prompts for Thinking About Science in Books: Jeanne Reardon developed a list of prompts to help students think about the science in books. Different prompts work in different ways depending on the focus of the lesson. It often works well to choose one prompt at a time and revisit different prompts throughout the year with a variety of books.

- What makes a book a science book?

- What does a science book do?

- How—in what ways—is this book a science book?

- What and/or how does the book make you wonder? What does it help you understand, think about, ask questions about?

- What kind of science did the author need to know to write this book?

- Reread your book and think about where the science is in this book. What kind of science is it? (Remember to make notes about pages and places in it to help you explain the book to the class.)

- What questions did the author have in her mind that she answered in this book? Are these important questions? Are these the same questions you have? What other questions might she have asked?

- What does the author think is important? What does he want you to think about?

- How does the author think like a scientist? How does this book make you think like a scientist?

- Does the author make any comparisons in this book? What kind? How do the comparisons help you think about science?

- Think about the connections in this book? Does the author make connections to other parts of science? Did you make any connections to other things you know? What kind of connections did you make?

- When a scientist reads this book what would the scientist notice? . . . think about? . . . look at? . . . talk about? How would a scientist read this book?

as a microscope to support his inquiry, changed and controlled variables as he redesigned his experiments, communicated his findings to a larger audience, and persevered in the face of constant failures. Brandon remarked, "Snowflake Bentley was a scientist just like we are." I asked students to reflect in their science journals on characteristics they have that they think help them to be good scientists.

Over the next few days, *Snowflake Bentley* circulated throughout the room. A waiting list was generated because so many students wanted to read the book again. During Science Workshop, as I observed groups of students working, I would occasionally hear the name Snowflake Bentley come up in discussion. Then one day, as I was reading Sasha's science journal, I noticed Snowflake Bentley in the text. We had been building straw structures as part of a unit on construction. She had written, "Our structure is still leaning. We tried to add more straws to the one side but they bent in the middle. We were going to give up and start over but Snowflake Bentley tried and tried and tried and he didn't give up so we're not going to either. Our plan for tomorrow is to try an X shape and see if it works." I began to realize that students were really identifying with Snowflake as a fellow scientist. He didn't look like the stereotypical scientist in the lab coat. His story made a real impression on them and made me realize that trade books about scientists and the work they do could contribute a great deal to students' scientific thinking.

I began to search for books written by or about scientists that told stories about their work. One particular favorite was *Project Puffin: How We Brought Puffins Back to Egg Rock* (1997) by Stephen W. Kress that tells the story of a wildlife scientist's efforts to reintroduce puffins to an island off the coast of Maine. What is so delightful about the book is that the scientist shares his own inquiry process from his initial questions to his next steps. Students were quick to note that he recorded his data and observations in a notebook just like they do.

Recommended Books written by or about scientists and their work

Once a Wolf: How Wildlife Biologists Fought to Bring Back the Gray Wolf by Stephen R. Swinburne.

This book tells the story of several wildlife scientists' efforts to reintroduce the gray wolf into the wilds of Yellowstone National Park.

Project Puffin: How We Brought Puffins Back to Egg Rock by Stephen W. Kress

Stephen Kress, a wildlife scientist, shares his story of how puffins were reintroduced to an island off the coast of Maine.

continued

Snowflake Bentley
by Jacqueline Briggs Martin

A biographical account of the life and work of Wilson Bentley, a Vermont farmer who spent his life studying and photographing snowflakes.

The Snake Scientist
by Sy Montgomery

An account of the research of Dr. Robert Mason, a zoologist, who studies red-sided garter snakes as they emerge each spring from winter caves in Canada.

Hidden Worlds: Looking Through a Scientist's Microscope
by Stephen Kramer

Explores the life and work of microscopist Dennis Kunkel who studies very tiny objects with a microscope.

Searching for Velociraptor
By Lowell Dingus and Mark A. Norell

Two paleontologists share the story of their search for and discovery of the fossilized remains of the dinosaur known as Velociraptor.

The Bones Detectives: How Forensic Anthropologists Solve Crimes and Uncover Mysteries of the Dead
By Donna M. Jackson

Explores the work of forensic scientists as they search for answers to unsolved mysteries.

Elephant Woman: Cynthia Moss Explores the World of Elephants
By Laurence Pringle

The story of zoologist Cynthia Moss who has dedicated her life to the study and protection of African elephants in Kenya.

Meeting Dolphins: My Adventures in the Sea
By Kathleen Dudzinski

Kathleen Dudzinski shares her story of how she became a wildife scientist and began a lifelong interest in researching dolphins.

What Is a Scientist?
By Barbara Lehn

A classroom of first-grade scientists share accounts of their investigations and explorations.

Over the next few weeks, through read-alouds and independent reading, students *met* scientists working under the sea, in the desert, and on the space shuttle. The work these scientists were doing, the questions they asked, and the methods of investigation they used validated the important work our students were doing in the classroom. Exploring the work of scientists through trade books not only put a new face on what a scientist looks like but also inspired our budding young scientists to continue their scientific endeavors.

Science-related trade books have supported, enriched, and inspired scientific explorations. Reading about the work of scientists and thinking about the science of communicating information through texts provided another rich layer to our understandings about how science works. This multiple-perspectives approach to literature left us not only better informed, but truly enlivened by our reading.

Although here I have mainly focused on the way science trade books enriched our scientific thinking, I would be remiss in not commenting on the many benefits science trade books bring to literacy development in general. The more trade books become an integral part of our science program, the more trade books become an integral part of our classroom. Instruction in one area often spills over into the domain of another. For example, a minilesson on what constitutes a good lead in a science book improves students' analytical skills. Work on ways to present data in context and how to take notes from texts offers big payoffs in writer's workshop. Strategies for reading information texts, using context clues to develop vocabulary, and sorting out fact and opinion are explored and reinforced in reader's workshop. Students can become familiar with the work of Jim Arnosky, Gail Gibbons, Seymour Simon, and Jean Craighead George through author studies and can use their newfound knowledge in discussions in their literature circles. As students evolve into more careful readers, as they interact more critically with trade books, both their science and literacy skills increase. It makes a kind of common sense.

References

Anderson, M. K. 1983. *Oil in Troubled Waters.* New York: Vanguard Press.

Carr, T. 1991. *Spill! The Story of the* Exxon Valdez. New York: Franklin Watts.

Dingus, L., and Norrell, M. A. 1996. *Searching for Velociraptor.* New York: HarperCollins.

Dudzinski, K. 2000. *Meeting Dolphins: My Adventures in the Sea.* Washington, DC: National Geographic Society.

Jackson, D. M. 1996. *The Bones Detectives: How Forensic Anthropologists Solve Crimes and Uncover Mysteries of the Dead*. New York: Little, Brown and Co.

Kramer, S. 2001. *Hidden Worlds: Looking Through a Scientist's Microscope*. New York: Houghton Mifflin.

Kress, S. W. 1997. *Project Puffin: How We Brought Puffins Back to Egg Rock*. Gardiner, ME: Tilbury House.

Lauber, P. 1986. *Volcano: The Eruption and Healing of Mount St. Helens*. New York: Bradbury Press.

Lehn, B. 1998. *What Is a Scientist?* Brookfield, CT: Millbrook Press.

Martin, J. B. 1998. *Snowflake Bentley*. Boston: Houghton Mifflin.

Montgomery, S. 1999. *The Snake Scientist*. Boston: Houghton Mifflin.

Pringle, L. 1997. *Elephant Woman: Cynthia Moss Explores the World of Elephants*. New York: Atheneum Books.

———. 1993. *Oil Spills: Damage, Recovery, and Prevention*. New York: Morrow.

Swinburne, S. R. 1999. *Once a Wolf: How Wildlife Biologists Fought to Bring Back the Gray Wolf*. Boston: Houghton Mifflin.

5 *Writing: A Way into Thinking Science*

Jeanne Reardon

Writing in science does more than provide a record of investigations and a way of collecting data for analysis and interpretation. Writing is a way into thinking science. While writing, child-scientists not only recount what they observed and did, but they also question, make connections, interpret, confirm or revise explanations, and plan next steps. As teachers, we can provide children with a framework for science writing, prompt them to push their thinking, and model how teacher-scientists write and use writing to think about and understand science.

This chapter is built on my experiences with student writers and my experiences while watching students learn science. Sometimes I will speak of reading, speaking, and listening as well as writing. It is the writing that ties the pieces together. In our classroom the act of writing is as common as greeting and talking with friends. We write lightly and playfully; we write seriously and thoughtfully; we write every day, and in every discipline. Often the very act of writing clarifies our understanding, but there is more. Writing is the way we think, organize, reflect, plan, and solve problems. Writing holds our thinking still so that we can revisit; rethink; and revise our plans, our conceptual understandings, our explanations, our theories.

What we write, when we write, and how we write are important, but the use we make of what we have written is equally important. I believe that students write so willingly during Science Workshop because they use what they write. During Science Workshop, I have never heard a student, even a fifth-grade student, ask, "How much do I have to write?" Writing is not viewed as an assignment; it is seen as valuable to students and to their classmates. It is essential to their inquiry. It is not possible to question, investigate, analyze data, and revise plans without written records.

Teachers' Writing in the Classroom

Before I describe students' science writing, I would like us to consider our writing—the teachers' writing. From reading Chapter 2, you know that I keep a journal. This is reflective writing that I do for my teaching-self, as contrasted to the observational writing and recordkeeping, example/ model writing, and writing to prompts that I do as part of my day-by-day teaching, and different still from the personal writing I do at home. My journal reflections are very important to me, but I know that not every-one is a journal writer or diary keeper. If you have never kept a teaching journal, you may want to try it. My advice is not to be slavishly rigid about making entries, but to be spontaneous and see how it goes. Journal writing is optional. Writing in the classroom is not optional, however. If we believe writing is essential to thinking, then we must write with and for the children in our classrooms.

Observational Notes

I make observational notes during the exploration/investigation part of Science Workshop and during Scientists' Meetings. These observations help me to maintain the course and energy of our Science Workshop, to plan minilessons, to identify needed resources, to consider writing prompts, and to assess and evaluate student learning. I have experi-mented with several different arrangements for recording my observa-tions and am still looking for the perfect one. My challenge is not in the making of observations, but in noting what I see in such a way that I can use my observations for multiple purposes.

   The observational form that I find most useful for planning is quite simple. I use a large spiral notebook and fold each page in half vertically. As I walk around and interact with the students during exploration/ investigation time, or listen during Scientists' Meetings, I make observa-tional notes on the left side. I include the names or initials of the students beside my observation. The right side is where I list needs, problematic areas, and possible solutions. As I read and reread my observations, I think about next steps: "Do students need some more examples of scien-tists' recordkeeping? Are there other materials that will assist them in finding solutions to their problems? Will using new materials challenge their existing explanations and push them to consider alternative expla-nations? Are there books, Internet sources, or people who can provide needed background information? Who can help Leigh and Roberto to more accurately read a thermometer? How can I best demonstrate cause-and-effect relationships? Whose data can I use to demonstrate looking for patterns? What questions can I ask to help students evaluate their explanations?"

   While this observation notebook is useful for planning and for assess-ing the class's progress toward inquiry and science knowledge goals, it is inadequate for assessing the progress of individual students. I find that I can reread my notes for evidence of some skills, abilities, and attitudes observed in students, but further observations of individual students are needed. So, in addition to my spiral notebook, I also maintain a looseleaf one with pages for each student. This is where I keep track of individual student progress. At the front of this notebook I keep my status-of-the-class records. This alphabetical list of student names and their plans for the next workshop was discussed in Chapter 2. I use this record sheet, together with students' Scientist's Notebooks and notes in my spiral notebook, to plan conferences and consultation meetings with students.

Teacher Modeling of Science Writing

Those of you who regularly write in front of the students as part of writing workshop understand the importance of demonstrating how you think as you write. When I model science writing, I write for a specific purpose and I draw on the explorations and investigations of students in the class. I write on chart paper and think aloud as I write.

Many students in our combined first/second-grade classroom were exploring questions related to a broad topic—"What is it about mittens that keeps your hands warm?" The students were at different places along the path of inquiry. Their questions reflected their growing ability to use observation to find questions that can lead to productive investigations—investigations that produce data to use in building explanations: "What's in mittens that keeps my hands warm? Are mittens always warm inside? Do mittens stay warm inside if they are empty—like when nobody's wearing them? How come wet mittens don't keep my hands warm? Do mittens keep the cold out or do they keep the hot in?" Many students were engaged in productive investigations and had recorded data in their Scientist's Notebooks. Several students had reported their explanations during a Scientists' Meeting. Now I wanted to demonstrate science thinking and writing that would show the relationship between evidence and explanations.

"Today we are going to work on writing that explains what is happening. We have to do two things: explain *what's going on* and tell *how we know*. Sometimes scientists call the "what's going on" sentence a claim. The how we know is called evidence. I want to write to explain how mittens keep my hands warm. My first sentence will be the claim that tells what's going on that causes mittens to keep hands warm. I'll write some of our ideas on the chalkboard. Next we'll look in our Scientist's Notebooks for evidence that supports the claim. If we find evidence I'll underline the claim sentence on the chalkboard."

To explain what was going on, students suggested that "Mittens are thick." "The stuff mittens are made out of keeps the cold from getting in.""Mittens make what's inside get hot.""Mittens keep your hands warm cause the warm can't get out."

I asked, "Did anyone do an investigation to show that mittens keep the cold from getting in?" Three children said they had and so they searched in their Scientist's Notebooks for what they did and the records of their findings. Then they underlined those parts of their notebooks. We did the same thing for each of the claims on the chalkboard, searching through notebooks and underlining anything we did that supported a claim. For some claims there were no investigations, for others there were investigations, but few records. Some children had done investigations and kept records. (We had to stop to discuss what we could do to show that mittens make what's inside them hot.)

Kevin had carried out several experiments where he put a thermometer in a mitten and closed the opening of the mitten with rubber bands. He had recorded the temperature on the thermometer before and after he put the mitten outside "for a while" and when he left the mitten in our room. He had also put a thermometer in his mitten and had worn his mitten with the thermometer in it when we went out for recess. Kevin's explanation for "how mittens keep your hands warm" was: "There is something in mittens that keeps the cold air from getting inside. Your hand is like a cork and keeps the air from getting in the open end."

I told the class, "We will be writing lots and lots of explanations about what we discover in Science Workshop. Today I am going to use Kevin's investigation to show how scientists write explanations. Kevin wants to explain how mittens keep your hands warm. Remember, I said that first scientists make a claim—what is happening, then they write the evidence—how they know that it is happening. The evidence is what they did and what they found that supports their claim. If there are findings that don't support their claim, scientists write that too. I'll write Kevin's claim on the chart. . . . Now I need to write the evidence. "What did Kevin do that shows something in mittens keeps the cold air from getting in?" I continued thinking aloud, asking the children questions and writing on the chart paper.

Writing in Response to Prompts

Another type of teacher writing is writing in response to the questions or prompts we give to students. We provide our students with questions to uncover their assumptions, to help them think about and understand how science works; to anticipate, introduce, focus on a new topic; to summarize; to identify and solve problems; and to assess and evaluate skills and conceptual understanding and knowledge. When we write with our students in response to prompts, we are pushed to thoughtfully consider the questions we ask. After writing our response, we are more curious about, and open to, the responses of others. I will elaborate on writing to prompts in the next section about students' writing.

Students' Writing During Science Workshop

Let's look first at student writing done within the Science Workshop, and then at science writing done outside of the structure of Science Workshop. As I discuss a variety of student science writing, I would like you to think about how often, and in how many ways, a single piece of writing is used by the author of a piece and her classmates.

In the Chapter 2 example of Science Workshop, I passed out Scientist's Notebooks the first day. That day the students wrote about what they had done and what they had observed during their exploration of building materials. They brought their pencils and Scientist's Notebooks with them to the first Scientists' Meeting. During the meeting, the students read and coded their entries with a *D* for something they did, an *O* for something they observed or noticed, and a *W* for something they wondered about. This helped them focus on one aspect of their exploration to share with others. After listening to other students' comments, they drew a line across the page to mark the end of their original entry, and then added anything that they wanted to try out for themselves, about which they wanted to find out more, or talk over with someone else. In this way, they were able to take advantage of their classmates' work and to plan for the next workshop.

The Scientist's Notebook provides each student with a record of his inquiries. It includes questions raised, questions answered, procedures followed, materials used, data collected and organized, references consulted, explanations generated, plans made, and personal reflections. The notebook is more than a collection of scientific drawings, tables, and charts, although those are included. It is a working document to be read and reread as the inquiry progresses. As such, it is part narrative; part lists and jottings of ideas; part numbers, symbols, drawings. The primary audience for this writing is the student scientist who is engaged in the inquiry. The Scientist's Notebook is a source of information to be used in discussions, and in writing expanded explanations, informative articles, and reports for the larger community of classroom scientists.

Setting Up and Using the Scientist's Notebook

I use legal size, unlined, white copy paper (8-1/2"-by-14"). A notebook is made of twenty to twenty-five sheets stapled together horizontally. The title, Scientist's Notebook, is written on the front cover, then the booklet is flipped over from bottom to top and ???? Plans is written on the back cover. Students work from both ends to the middle of their Scientist's Notebooks. Questions are central to inquiry and although questions appear within the routine entries, as students work from the front of the notebooks, it is important to have a place to record questions whenever they come to mind. I have noticed that students often write questions in the back of their notebooks during Scientists' Meetings while listening to other students report on work. Students often fill several notebooks during a school year.

Before students make entries in their journal, they fold under 1-1/2 to 2 inches from the right edge of the page. When unfolded, this provides space for children to react and respond to their work; to write comments, ideas, explanations, plans for future explorations. . . . Some students make drawings for next steps, some make comments inside conversation bubbles: "Starts here—the real explanation." I once had a student who left a margin on the left side as well as the right. She would ask questions about the investigation on the left—"Where did you hold the flashlight? How come the shadow's so long?" She would answer herself in the right margin—"I better measure and draw the flashlight. Good question—don't know." Scientist's Notebook writing is single-draft writing and we need to have space available to react to our work at the place of response rather than beginning a new page at the end. It is essential to have this wide empty margin.

If children are exploring, I ask them to stop every ten or fifteen minutes to "Write what you did . . . what you noticed . . . what you wonder about . . . anything that surprises you." Children use drawings, lists, phrases, sentences, charts, conversation bubbles, . . . to record what they are exploring and thinking. If students are investigating a question, then they record as they work. While students are investigating, I stop by to watch and ask, "How will you record what is happening, what you see? What are you writing to show how much . . ., how long . . ., the procedure you used . . .?" When students are first introduced to Science Workshop, they often become so involved in their investigation that they forget to make records. When I see a student recording his measurements, procedures, findings . . ., as he works I will call, "Stop and come over for a minute" (see Chapter 2). Everyone comes over to look at and to talk over the entry with the student.

Since my retirement a year and half ago I no longer have student notebooks to show you. The example in Figure 5–1 is based on my notes from a writing across the curriculum presentation I made to the staff in my school. It is typical of a first-grade student's notebook including the sentence fragments and misspelled words. The student is the audience for his Scientist's Notebook writing. It is not written for the teacher or for a distant audience needing detailed background information. This is not a time for complete sentences and corrected spelling, but for keeping track of ideas, observations, actions taken, and reactions.

My notes indicate that the student had been talking with his class-mates about his idea that the stuff mittens are made of keeps the cold from getting in. (We would probably think of this as the insulation

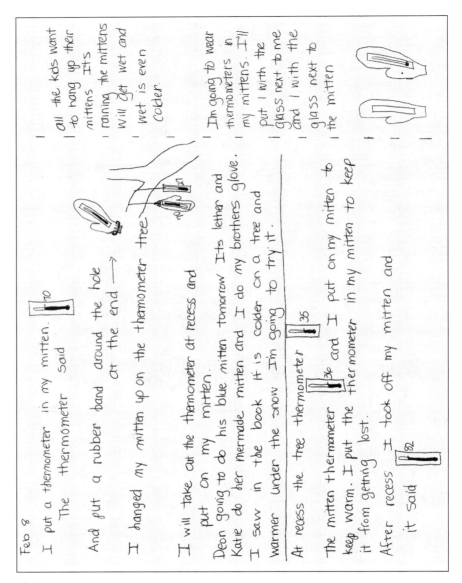

Figure 5–1.

theory.) He did not record the material of his mitten, but later notes the blue leather of Deon's mitten and Katie's mermaid mitten. He records the details he thinks will be important: the temperature of the room (and his mitten), closing the opening with a rubber band, the temperature of the air outside. He notes that the mitten with the thermometer will hang outside until recess. After hanging up his mitten, the author joins his classmates' conversation. Katie has noticed that when she first gets in bed it is really cold, no matter how many blankets. Later on she gets hot. Deon thinks maybe the temperature in the mitten hanging outside will go down first, then go up just like in bed. The entry states that Deon is going to do his blue mitten tomorrow. It's leather. . . . Next comes another planning entry. The student will try for himself to see if the temperature of the soil under the snow is warmer than the air. I clearly remember when he talked about this in Scientists' Meeting, and I was amazed when he made a connection between the snow keeping the cold out and his mitten keeping the cold out.

The line drawn across the page shows the end of the morning investigation. After lunch recess the student records his findings: the temperature of the air outside and the temperature inside his mitten. He also writes that he put on his mitten with the thermometer in it, and records the temperature shown on the thermometer when he gets back in after recess—after he had been wearing the thermometer.

Earlier I noted that the space made available by folding over the edge of the page could be used for different purposes. I may direct the students to read entries and to code for observations, or procedures followed, or for evidence. Other times I may direct the students to read and reread their entries thinking as scientists and then write what they are thinking. On the day of this entry, my directions were probably to read what you wrote, then think about what it means and what you will do next.

In the fold-over space, this student notes that others want to do what he has done. (Students often include social comments in their notebooks.) He also starts a whole new idea about wet being even colder and wrote this comment in the back of his notebook as something he wanted to investigate later. The class became very curious about the temperature of wet and dry mittens. Perhaps the student is beginning to think about the effect of the warmth of his hand on the temperature in the mitten and so he plans his next step. The thermometers we use in our room have the glass column stapled to a cardboard or plastic backing. He is going to put one thermometer in his mitten with the glass column next to his skin and in his other mitten he will have the plastic or paper next to his skin.

It is important to have space for thoughts while rereading notes. I find that when students have space available for writing reactions and responses they think and rethink their investigations.

Drawings, Charts, Diagrams, Graphs, and More

It is important for the student to decide when, for what purpose, and in what form she will record information. Too often students are provided with an empty form to use for recording information without a discussion of the purpose of that particular representation. Some forms are better for recording observations, some are better for collecting or analyzing data, others are better for communicating findings. When the teacher provides the table or chart to be filled in, students' thinking is restricted and alternatives are lost. I remember a first-grade child placing a variety of objects in a clear plastic aquarium and watching the materials sink or float. During Scientists' Meeting she shared the chart she had constructed to record her observations. Her chart listed the objects she used along the left side, but rather than the usual headings of sink or float, she had three categories: *sink, float,* and *strange.* She told the class that *strange* was for objects that didn't sink and rest on the bottom, but floated part way down, or objects that floated for a while and then sank, or sank after she dropped water on them. She added that she planned to investigate the strange ones. We need to read, discuss, and analyze the drawings, tables, charts, graphs, and diagrams found in books and news and scientific articles. A student who has experience reading, analyzing, and using a variety of representational forms is better able to select or create a form that serves her purpose.

Coding Entries

Before coming to Scientists' Meetings the students date and reread their entries. I may direct them to code their entries to facilitate thinking and discussion. Recall that in Chapter 2 I asked the students to use letter codes to mark their notebooks after rereading, "*D* for something you did, *O* if it is something you observed, and *W* if it's something you wonder about." Sometimes I have the students code with letters and other times I ask them to underline. If children are having a difficult time distinguishing between observations and comments, I say, "Reread what you wrote today and underline what you noticed—observed with your senses—with a red pencil. Underline any comments you wrote with a blue pencil." When we meet, we discuss both comments and observations. Comments help children make connections and build explanations, but they are not the same as observations. Other times I may have students underline procedures they used, explanations, evidence, or something they found surprising. Then we focus our discussion on the aspect of their work that they have been asked to underline.

Additional Thoughts

During Scientists' Meetings, three or four children report on their work and lead the follow-up discussion. Other children offer questions, suggestions, challenges. After each discussion there is time for students to enter additional thoughts, questions, plans, ideas in their notebooks. In science we want students to adopt a speculative stance. Providing time to make additional entries after discussion helps students realize the tentative and unfinished nature of scientific knowledge and understandings.

Scientist's Notebooks are used at other times during the day outside the Science Workshop structure. The notebook often becomes the text for reading groups or a resource for expanded writing. We read notebooks in small groups or during whole-class lessons to look for implied questions, to plan for or refine our testing of hunches, to share ways to find answers to questions, to discuss the significance of surprises, to settle on a common vocabulary, and/or to make connections to other work.

Prompts for Writing

Frequently I provide the class with a question or prompt to write to. You may recall from Chapter 2 that I gave the children a prompt to write to before our first Science Workshop when I asked: "What do you think will happen when we have science workshop this afternoon? Take a few minutes to think and write down your ideas." Sometimes we write at the beginning of Science Workshop, to bring prior experiences and understandings to the surface or to identify and consider a problem. We may write at the end of an exploration/investigation time to summarize or reflect on some aspect of our work. Sometimes we write after Scientists' Meetings to uncover assumptions about how science works or to assess knowledge and understanding.

Over the years I have compiled a collection of prompts that I find effective in assisting students in their inquiries and in developing their understanding of the ways of science. These are some of the questions that help us think about our own inquiry processes:

- What surprised you?

- What are you wondering?

- Where do your questions come from?

- What makes a good question?

- How do you decide what to record?

- How do you use your Scientist's Notebook?

- What are you doing when you are doing science?

- How do you know when to stop investigating, that is, know that you are finished?

- Do you ever give up on, abandon, your idea/question/explanation? Why? When?

- How do you decide if an explanation is a good explanation? What makes one explanation better than another?

- If someone asked you to help write an explanation, what would you do, that is, how would you help?

- What makes you revise your explanation?
- What kind of evidence do you find convincing?
- What do you do when you get stuck?
- How do you decide what to do next?

When students write and share responses to these kinds of prompts, it makes the thinking of all the scientists in the room available to everyone. It gives students new ways of thinking about and doing science, and provides an opportunity for them to assess their own understanding of the inquiry process.

After we have written in response to a question, we discuss not only the content of our response, but how the particular question pushed our thinking. Later, I shorten the prompt to a stem and then add it to a chart I call "Writing to Think and Learn in Science." Students often refer to this chart when they are writing their unprompted reflections at the end of an exploration/investigation time. In the following lists, I have grouped some of the stems I use by the purpose they fulfill.

Focusing, Anticipating, Introducing

- What is _____? (Fill in with a topic you will begin studying— What is electricity? . . . a material? . . . a tool? . . . a concept? . . .)
- Write three (five) things you know (believe) about _____. (electricity, friction, . . .)
- What are you doing when you are _____? (lifting a heavy object, . . .)

When we share responses to these stems, I find out where the students are, what they already know and understand, their misconceptions or confusions. Using this information, we are able to identify experts in the class who can assist us in our study.

Learning Something New, Making Connections, and Summarizing

- What I discovered/learned about_____.
- How _____ fits in with what I already know about _____.
- What I think about _____.
- I think _____ means.
- This is my definition of _____.
- I could teach someone about / how to / how to use a _____.

Coupling the introducing stems with these stems provides a basis for comparison and a way to document change in students' knowledge and understanding.

Problem or Question Identification

- I was surprised when_____.
- This is the problem I had when I _____.
- think my problem is _____.
- Some questions I have (still have) about _____ are _____.
- The problem I had doing _____ is _____.

Problem Solving and Assessment

- This is how I solved the problem _____.
- The procedure I used to _____ is _____.
- My rule for _____ is _____.
- My idea about why _____ happens is _____.
- This is how I know that _____.

Writing Outside of Science Workshop

The science writing I have discussed so far has been single-draft writing done by students during Science Workshop. This writing helps students pursue their inquiry questions and construct explanations based on their investigations. Students also need opportunities to write longer pieces such as expanded explanations, reports, informative articles, and writing to encourage action. I find that writing workshop is the place to write longer pieces because its structure provides the necessary time, support, and responses for such writing.

The example I gave of modeling explanation writing took place during science workshop; it was single-draft writing aimed at understanding the relationship of explanation and evidence, not writing for publication. We work on expanded explanations, the kind that can be published, during writing workshop. These explanations are discussed in response groups, revised, edited, and prooofread before they are published and shared with a wider audience.

Reports are one way to communicate information to a wide audience. Students engaged in inquiry generate findings and make claims based on their investigations. Older students need to compare their work with published material, consider claims and/or arguments that support or disagree with theirs and think about the basis for the agreement or disagreement. Reports for Scientists' Meetings require students to organize their work for an audience of their classmates. Students need to read reports of practicing scientists to see how they are written and to think about what to include and how to present data and findings.

I have found that often the short scientific research articles, which appear in a weekly science news magazine—for example, *Science News*—provide a good basis for discussion and analysis of a report. This particular magazine is written for adults, but I have used articles with fourth- and fifth-grade students. I just read a report about the cognitive capacity of jays entitled "Birds with a Criminal Past Hide Food Well" (Milius 2001). In addition to findings, this brief article includes other information such as: "The experiment grew out of some big questions about the capacities of animal cognition, as well as Clayton's lunching habits during a year in California, where scrub jays forage for crumbs. Several times Clayton noticed what she later observed in the lab" (p.325). Tests are described and connections are made to other research: "Emery draws evidence to challenge longtime assumptions about animal cognition. For years people have assumed . . ." (p. 325). It is a good idea to collect articles written by professional science writers for use with students who are writing science reports.

I have also worked with fourth- and fifth-grade students on other kinds of science writing, including writing about controversies and to encourage action. Controversial science issues are national and international in scope; several come to mind immediately: global warming, genetically altered food, and stem cell research. I recently discovered the K through 12 SCOPE (Science Controversies: On-Line Partnerships in Education) website *http://scope.educ.washington.edu/*. The site focuses on scientific controversies with descriptions for in-school projects. Students are encouraged to take a position on a given issue, and then to investigate the pros and cons of their position through guided activities and web research. Students who participate in these projects write as they research to support an opinion.

Writing to encourage action is persuasive writing about an issue of importance to the class and relevant to an authentic community problem. When the declining frog population in our creeks was publicized, we began investigating local pollution and ways to lessen the effects of water pollution in our community. Writing to encourage action about issues requires scientific knowledge as well as an understanding of persuasive writing.

I have not discussed all of the science-related writing that is done by students. Students' writing is strongly influenced by their reading, so it is important to have a wide variety of written texts, photographs, and other media available for them. Science articles from the popular press, journal articles, information books or trade books written about a single topic, papers and notebooks of practicing scientists, identification guides, photo essays, reference books, articles found on the Internet all provide useful text to familiarize students with the discourse of science. Students must read widely and discuss what they read in order to distinguish scientific and nonscientific ideas, to recognize facts and opinions, to have examples of ways to represent data and findings, to evaluate practices—to become science writers.

The science of our Science Workshops—the students' scientific awareness and their wide reading—is apparent in their writing. There is always a large collection of poetry books in our classroom and children frequently write poems that reflect their close observation of the world and their engagement with science. After a book of superstitions made its way around the classroom, I noticed students writing science superstitions. Students often use science-based similes and metaphors in their writing. Reviews of science trade books and science television shows regularly appear on our classroom message board. Some may not consider this to be science writing but much of the writing I see is clearly informed by close observation of natural phenomena and a burgeoning knowledge of science.

I began this chapter saying, "Writing is a way into thinking science." Writing is the way we think, organize, reflect, plan, and solve problems. Writing holds our thinking still so that we can revisit, rethink, and revise our plans, our conceptual understandings, our explanations, our theories. In conclusion I would add, writing does all of that and more—it puts us in touch with the beauty of science.

References

Milius, S. 2001. "Birds with a Criminal Past Hide Food Well." *Science News*, 160 (21): 325.

Further Reading

Duckworth, E. 1996. *The Having of Wonderful Ideas and Other Essays on Teaching and Learning*. New York: Teachers College Press.

Feely, J. 1993. "Writing in Science." In *Science and Language Links: Classroom Implications,* edited by J. Scott. Portsmouth, NH: Heinemann.

Fletcher, R., and J. Portalupi. 2001. *Writing Workshop: The Essential Guide*. Portsmouth, NH: Heinemann.

———. 2001. *Nonfiction Craft Lessons*. Portland, ME: Stenhouse.

Graves, D. 1994. *A Fresh Look at Writing.* Portsmouth, NH: Heinemann.

Hansen, J. 1987. *When Writers Read.* Portsmouth, NH: Heinemann.

Harvey, S. 1998. *Nonfiction Matters.* Portland, ME: Stenhouse.

Hines, P. 2001. "Why Controversy Belongs in the Science Classroom." *Harvard Education Letter* (17) (2) 8.

Lindfors, J. 1999. *Children's Inquiry: Using Language to Make Sense of the World.* New York: Teachers College Press.

6 *Inquiring into Assessment*

Donna Dieckman

Evaluation ought to be one of the greatest energy givers for the teacher in the classroom.

—Donald Graves (2001, p. 82.)

Testing, norm-based . . . reference-based . . . standards-based . . . research-based . . . performance-based—my friend Wendy Saul worries that these words are "exploding in teachers' ears like friendly fire from some low-flying bomber." Whose job is it to gather intelligence, to ask if this heavy barrage is really resulting in better instruction and increased learning? Do we wish to rely solely on reports from the "air" or should we also be gathering information about classroom life from the ground?

Here is what every good teacher knows: the purpose and real pleasure of teaching comes from helping students learn. There are few things more exhilarating than seeing growth in our students and few things more demoralizing than being unable to help a child who seems "stuck." So why that feeling of attack? What is the relationship between an individual teacher's interest in student growth and achievement and the current nationwide emphasis on assessment and evaluation? Let's consider a few propositions that make sense from a teacher's point of view.

1. Good teachers closely and frequently monitor the progress of their students and adjust instructional plans to meet students' needs.

2. A significant statistical relationship between a specific program and student achievement is not enough for a good teacher. While an 80 percent success rate would be great in a published account of educational progress, a teacher is responsible for 100 percent of the children in her class.

3. Good teachers begin with the students they have, not with the students they wished they had. It is senseless for a teacher to follow a curriculum that his students cannot follow.

4. Tests should be read as statements about what a district or nation believes is important to teach. Teachers, parents, and students need to examine the assessment tests being used and talk about them in curricular terms.

5. Teachers need evidence if they are to argue for a particular kind of instruction.

Although most of the remainder of this chapter presents ways that teachers can monitor student progress to improve instruction, it seems useful to begin with large-scale data that school-based folks can use as they argue for the kind of instruction advocated in this book.

Large-Scale Evidence

Numbers, which seek to describe student achievement, now appear regularly in our nation's newspapers and by the time this book is reprinted, these numbers will be replaced by new numbers. Make no mistake, it is important for large units like governments to monitor trends. There are two questions key to the interpretation of these numbers: (1) what tests are used to gather the data (i.e., do we believe that what is being tested is in fact a measure of what will enable students to succeed) and (2) what questions are the data being used to answer?

For instance, in the state of Maryland we had a performance-based interdisciplinary test that sought to measure a student's ability to read for understanding, to write coherently and effectively, and to gather information and use it appropriately. Looking at the data garnered from this test, it was relatively easy to compare school districts—expenditures per pupil, teacher salary and education, curricular decisions, and so forth.

These tests did not tell us much, however, about the effect on student achievement of long-term teacher development efforts. They also didn't let us sort, within schools, to see if improvements in test scores were coming from children who were already doing well and are now doing better, or if they reflected improvements in the skills of the children most likely to be left behind.

In Eastern Europe, for instance, test scores have traditionally been quite high, especially when considered in light of their socioeconomic circumstances. These results cause us to ask several intriguing questions: Are the high scores the result of a difference in attitudes toward school or a difference in the curriculum? Are these students able to do as well later in their careers as students who have had significantly more lab experience and less memory work (and perhaps didn't score quite as well)? What population does the test report about (e.g., what percentage of students, for instance, are in school during the year the test is given)? The point here is that a much more *nuanced* discussion of test results is necessary in order to make sense of the numbers provided. But *nuanced*, does not make for great sound bites. It's a real problem.

One of the most interesting data sets comes from superintendent of schools Mike Klentschy, El Centro school district in southeast California.

The 6,542 students attending the eleven Title 1 El Centro schools are 82 percent Hispanic, 12 percent Caucasian, 3 percent African American, and 3 percent Asian American. A total of 52 percent of the students are Limited English Proficient and 73 percent of all students qualify for free or reduced lunches. The El Centro school district piloted a local systemic change initiative to improve science education that now includes all fourteen school districts in the Imperial Valley.

The science program, based on the LASER Model for systemic reform developed by the National Science Resources Center, includes five essential elements (NAS 1997):

1. High-quality curriculum

2. Sustained professional development

3. Materials support

4. Community and administrative support

5. Assessment and evaluation

Various formative and summative assessments, including performance assessments are used as part of the three or four *kit-based* units of study.

In addition, standardized tests are used to compare student data to national samples. Standardized test results from El Centro's Grades 4 and 6 (Stanford Achievement Test, Ninth Edition, Form T—Science Section) indicate a steady improvement in student science achievement based on the years of participation in the science program, as shown in Table 6–1. While science improvement might be expected from an effective reform initiative, what is most interesting are the results of the reading standardized tests shown in Table 6–2 (Stanford Achievement Test, Ninth Edition, Form T—Reading Section) and a sixth-grade writing proficiency assessment (see Table 6–3). These tests indicate a similar improvement in reading and writing achievement for students who participated in the science program. Analysis of student data to determine possible effects on math achievement is currently underway.

What might explain these results across the curriculum? A closer look at the initiative reveals the use of science trade books and student notebooks as integral components of the inquiry-based science program. Students are not only engaged in hands-on experiences, but they are reading, writing, and communicating science as part of their investigations. In an era when science is literally being tossed from the curriculum in favor of more work in reading, this data suggests a potential connection between inquiry-based science programs and reading and writing achievement. If reading skill is, in fact, the ability to make meaning from text, it is not totally surprising that a content-rich program would help students with comprehension-based activities.

Table 6–1. Stanford Achievement Test, Ninth Edition, Form T—Science Section
Spring 1999 Results in Mean National Percentiles: Grades 4 and 6
Disaggregated by Years of Student Participation in District Science Program

Years of Participation	Grade 4 Cumulative Mean (NPR = 36)		Grade 6 Cumulative Mean (NPR = 40)	
	NPR	N	NPR	N
Year O	21	137	27	174
Year l	32	149	32	121
Year 2	38	142	42	132
Year 3	47	111	50	107
Year 4	53	91	64	104

Table 6–2. Stanford Achievement Test, Ninth Edition, Form T—Reading Section
Spring 1999 Results in Mean National Percentile Scores: Grades 4 and 6
Disaggregated by Years of Student Participation in District Science Program

Years of Participation	Grade 4 Cumulative Mean(NPR = 33)		Grade 6 Cumulative (Mean NPR = 40)	
	NPR	N	NPR	N
Year O	23	137	25	174
Year l	27	149	28	121
Year 2	44	142	41	132
Year 3	42	111	49	107
Year 4	57	91	67	104

Table 6–3. Grade 6 Writing Proficiency Pass Rate
Spring 1999 Administration
Disaggregated by Years of Participation in District Science Program

Years of Participation	Pass Rate (Percent)	Number Tested
Cumulative	71	636
0	25	158
1	58	144
2	73	122
3	88	114
4	94	98

Monitoring Comprehension in Science

What strategies can we use to understand more about students' comprehension of science? What evidence can we garner about what and how students have learned? These are teacher questions as opposed to the kind of large-scale questions the preceding data seeks to answer. As teachers, we approach these queries with the same methods and processes we use in other scientific inquiries—we collect and analyze data.

There are many tools and resources that help us gather data to use in assessing students' understanding of science; tools, including the following, also enable us to share information about learner attitudes and thinking:

- Methods to systematically record observations of student work and conversations

- Visual organizers that teachers and students can use to monitor progress and plan next steps

- Collections of student work that tell a story over time

- Formal assessments that allow students to demonstrate understanding through engaging in problem-solving tasks

All of these resources provide data to analyze. Together students and teachers can look for evidence that indicates growth and understanding.

Checklists and Rating Scales

A *checklist* is a written description of observable behaviors or criteria. Copies of the desirable behaviors are distributed and students and teachers use them as a site for providing evidence that they are able to perform the behavior in question and the date on which the entry is made. Checklists can be simple—the user simply checks off a box to indicate the attainment of a specific skill or process—or can be slightly nuanced by adding frequency descriptors (Often, Sometimes, Seldom, Never) or numerical ratings (1–5). See Figure 3–12 in this book for an example developed by Charles Pearce.

Jeanne Reardon suggests another possibility: leave lines after each indicator and then record the date of the observation and the relevant behavior that was noted next to the indicator. For example, next to the "Asks testable questions" line, the teacher writes: 9/23, SJ (SJ for science journal) or 11/14, SJ; or next to the "Reads for additional information related to an investigation" line, she writes: 9/29, MC (MC for media center) or 9/30, WWW, and so forth.

Anecdotal Records

Anecdotal records offer recorded observations of student behaviors throughout the year. Teachers look for evidence and take notes either while students are working in groups or individually. Observation notes usually include the date since we are always interested in growth over time and the consistency of the behaviors in question. The record is basically written to describe what happened and under what circumstances. Anecdotal records can be collected in a variety of ways and are helpful for looking for patterns of student behavior. Some teachers keep a notebook or binder with sections or pages that include notes about each student. Others use sticky notes to record observations and later transfer these notes to a folder that is kept on each student.

Science-Talk Observations

If we are to understand students' science thinking, we must listen closely to their conversations and discussions with their fellow students; it is not enough to assess just the products of their investigations. While it is easier to collect students' work samples than to collect their talk, it is often in science talk that we find evidence of scientific reasoning. Jeanne Reardon frequently makes audio tapes of Scientists' Meetings so that she can replay and focus on particular student understandings and behaviors. She may listen for responses to explanations, for questions and follow-up questions, or for connections made to work done by others (students or practicing scientists). Records of conversations and discussions during investigations are made on sticky notes and then added to a loose-leaf notebook with sections for data collected about each student.

Questionnaires and Surveys

Questionnaires and surveys are helpful in assessing students' interests and attitudes about science. Questions may be open-ended or students may be asked to rate their responses to specific statements. A Likert scale, which uses a five-point rating from (5) strongly agree to (1) strongly disagree, is often used here. Figure 6–1 shows a students' survey designed by Charles Pearce (1999). Questionnaires and surveys are also beneficial for students as they consider their own level of participation in a given activity or group project. Such scales also allow them to easily voice their concerns and opinions about specific issues.

Interviews and Student Conferences

The term *interview* generally conjures up an image of one person who questions, most often the teacher, and another who responds, usually the student, though in practice they need not be so formal. Oral and written interviews are an effective means of assessing a student's understanding of inquiry science.

Student Survey

Name _____

Read each statement and circle the appropriate response.

SA: strongly agree   A: agree   D: disagree   SD: strongly disagree   N: no opinion

1. Learning is boring.   SA A   D SD N
2. I learn best by reading chapters and answering questions.   SA A   D SD N
3. As I learn, it is important to think about my thinking.   SA A   D SD N
4. I learn more if I have a choice about what I will be learning.   SA A   D SD N
5. When I talk things over with my partner I understand more about what I am learning.   SA A   D SD N
6. I learn more when I work in a group and share ideas.   SA A   D SD N
7. Discovering answers to my own questions is interesting.   SA A   D SD N
8. The best way to measure learning is for my teacher to give tests.   SA A   D SD N
9. My teacher can measure my learning by reading my journal.   SA A   D SD N
10. I like to discuss what I have discovered.   SA A   D SD N
11. Learning is finding out about things that interest me.   SA A   D SD N
12. Learning about science is only important for kids who want to become scientists.   SA A   D SD N
13. I am a scientist.   SA A   D SD N
14. I enjoy reading science picture books.   SA A   D SD N
15. A scientist asks questions.   SA A   D SD N
16. Science textbooks are the best books to read to learn about science.   SA A   D SD N
17. Scientists should answer old questions before asking new ones.   SA A   D SD N
18. I can learn more by reading than by doing.   SA A   D SD N
19. Facts I discover on my own are more memorable than facts someone tells me.   SA A   D SD N
20. Reading, math, and social studies are all parts of science.   SA A   D SD N
21. What do you think science really is? (use the back for more space)

Figure 6–1. A sample Student Survey form

Interviews can be held in conjunction with a checklist such as the one in Figure 3–12 (p. 70). In this case, the teacher schedules a student interview that focuses on six to eight items from the checklist. It works well to select four items that the teacher has observed often and two that the teacher has not observed. The student prepares for the interview by collecting evidence to document the items selected.

Before holding the first interview it is helpful to model the interview process in front of the class . . . in a kind of fishbowl arrangement. A six-item interview usually takes eight to ten minutes. It is important to interview each student several times during the year, but interviews do not need to be reserved for the end of the grading period. Once the first round of interviews is complete and students are familiar with the process, students can interview one another. The interview records become part of the data used to assess individual and class progress.

Conferences engage us in a slightly different dialogue, one that leaves room for clarification of understandings and expectations, and for planning as well as responding to the assessment questions. During the thirty-five to forty-five minute Science Workshop investigation time, Jeanne Reardon makes observational notes and has conferences with students as well as supports their inquiries. She uses variations or modifications of the Science Conference form shown in Figure 6–2 at all grade levels, selecting items developmentally appropriate to the students. This form is constructed with the students slowly, item by item, as the ways of science and scientists are discussed during minilessons and practiced by the students during their investigations.

Jeanne considers the collaborative construction of a conference form to be a critical part of students' learning. The form provides students with a guide to the way science is practiced by scientists in the larger community. She plans time for one ten- to twelve-minute conference during every Science Workshop. Just as in interviews the student prepares for the conference by considering and gathering evidence relevant to the selected item(s). Because this is a conference, it should be a time to provide opportunities for both the student and teacher to explore the topic and to request clarification, examples, and further possibilities—Teacher: "Let's talk about questions first. Where do your questions come from, when do you ask questions?" Student: "I have a hard time coming up with the right little questions while I'm investigating the big question."

In a primary classroom Jeanne tells the student what will be discussed at the conference. Together they look for evidence in the student's Scientist's Notebook and in Jeanne's loose-leaf notebook. For example, a kindergarten student's conference may focus on questions asked and records of observations. Together they would look for questions in the student's notebook and on Jeanne's sticky notes, questions in response to observations, to read-alouds, to other students' reports of their work, and

SCIENCE CONFERENCE

Name: **Date:**

Questions:

- Prompted by observations, curiosity, confusions, unanticipated findings, explanations, tests, data
- About own work, work of others, reading
- During minilessons, explorations/investigations, scientists' meetings, conversations, and discussions

Scientist's Notebook:

- Includes questions, scientific drawings, data collections, observations, descriptions of procedures, lists, comments, plans, tests, reflections, response to prompts
- Used to ask new questions, record data, describe procedures, build explanations, plan next steps of investigation, make connections, report work in progress

Explanations:

- Based on evidence from investigations, resources
- Compared to current thinking of science
- Revised in response to new evidence
- Considers other possible explanations
- Written, presented to class, respond to questions and comments

Explorations and Investigations:

- Records work in scientist's notebook
- Uses tools and/or scientific instruments
- Knows and uses several ways of recording and analyzing data
- Builds on the work of others
- Describes investigations in a way that others can replicate

Resources:

- Uses books, magazines, news articles, people, materials, WWW
- Used for wide reading, background information, models, to confirm or discredit findings and explanations
- Evaluation based on publication date, credibility of author

Scientists' Meetings:

- Reports work in progress, findings, explanations
- Considers classmates response to own work
- Listens and responds to other students' work

Plans:

Figure 6–2. A sample Science Conference form.

so forth. They would also look at writings and drawings done during explorations and investigations. At the conclusion of the conference, they would plan for a specific change—in the kinds of questions, in record-keeping, or an entirely different focus.

These conference records and the collection of observational notes for each student (see Chapter 5) are the data Jeanne uses for assessment. For older students, her notes include assessment of content knowledge as well as inquiry behaviors. Each conference ends with the student and the teacher planning for one area to focus on during the coming weeks.

Collections of Student-Authored Work

Students' written work is an important source of data; many examples are described in Chapters 2, 3, and 5. Whether called scientists' note-books, science journals, or discovery logs, these records of student inquiries are a rich source of data for assessing students' scientific think-ing, and understanding the inquiry process, procedures, and methods they use for science. More formal reports, written explanations, journal articles, or informative essays, as discussed in Chapter 5, contribute another perspective and add to this data collection. The student writing found on bulletin boards, the question board, and message boards are yet another source of data. If you teach the same students all day, then you will also have student writings across the curriculum. A writing folder for each student also provides the teacher with a rich source of data to analyze.

Portfolios

Portfolios are a purposeful, organized collection of students' work that document thinking, understanding, and growth over a period of time. Ideally, portfolios should be works-in-progress and need to be main-tained throughout the year. Students reflect on, select, and evaluate products and other artifacts that they feel best represent their meaning-ful learning experiences. Teachers can learn a great deal from analyzing the selections students make and can gain insight by closely reading stu-dent self-assessments. Students learn that their work tells a story that changes and grows throughout the year and that is an integral part of the learning process.

Assessments of Science Knowledge

As Charles Pearce notes in Chapter 3, most science curricula provide a means for testing and assessing knowledge. Teachers can also make up their own tests to assess specific knowledge related to a topic or unit of study. Several of Jeanne Reardon's prompts (see Chapter 5) can also be used to assess science knowledge: "I think *reflect* means . . ."; "My definition of *a symbiotic relationship* is . . .”; “This is how I know that *an object is vibrating . . .*”

One of the most authentic kinds of assessment, and one that might now privilege one way of knowing over another, is what is called performance assessment. *Performance assessments* are tasks that engage students in meaningful, real-world problem-solving experiences. As opposed to traditional tests that have preordained correct answers and finite application opportunities, performance assessments integrate content and process in interdisciplinary, open-ended tasks. Instead of factual recall, emphasis is placed on critical thinking. Performance assessments provide opportunities for students to demonstrate science process skills as well as write about their scientific understanding in a variety of ways.

Assessment as Part of the Inquiry Process

While all these assessment tools are helpful to teachers and students for data collection and analysis, there is yet another vital role assessment plays in the classroom. In addition to being a means of documenting and monitoring progress, assessment is also a critical part of the inquiry process. Again, I return to a classroom story to explain.

When I first began to think about how an inquiry-based approach to science might work in our classroom, my own concerns centered around helping kids to ask good questions, the management of materials, and what I could do to build a classroom community of scientists. I understood little about how assessment would fit into the process.

I did, however, have several tried-and-true assessment tools in place and assumed that I would use these to monitor student activities and behaviors. It made sense that observation checklists, anecdotal records, and informal conferences would be helpful. I used a laminated file folder with students’ names to jot down observations on sticky notes to be transferred later to individual student folders. I used these observations to look for patterns and to pinpoint individual student’s needs and strengths. I also planned to use science journals as written records of our Science Workshop activities; in this way, I could track students’ ability to formulate questions, record and analyze data, and so forth. Our journals were simply sheets of blank paper stapled together with a construction paper cover that were used to record student work over a period of time. I was comfortable and familiar with these assessment tools since I had used them in various ways throughout the day in our classroom.

It wasn’t until our class embarked on our first authentic inquiry investigating oil spills (see Chapter 4 for the story) that I began to understand how important assessment is in the inquiry process. Again, it was my students who taught me this lesson. From the very beginning of our investigations when students were gathering background information and working in teams to develop investigative procedures, questions arose about how we would evaluate our procedures. Students are very conscious of the concept of *fair* and readily applied this to the work we were doing. Our discussions began to focus less and less on the finished product and more and more on the process.

This first became clear when we began to formulate plans for cleaning up the oil that we had spilled during our simulation. Since each team would be making its own plan, questions arose about how individual teams would evaluate the success of the materials they used and how we, as a class, could share and compare data. It became apparent that there needed to be some standards and controls in place before proceeding to creating clean-up plans. How could we *fairly* compare one material to another if, at the same time, we were trying to judge the success of our efforts?

Consensus was reached, after much discussion—we needed to revise our original plans for the investigation. Students decided that instead of every group developing their own simulation materials, it would be more effective if we, as a class, developed simulation materials and made them available for everyone to use as a base for their planning and investigation. Students formed groups in order to research and develop various materials. Once the class agreed on the clean-up materials to be used, the students resumed planning.

The most difficult decisions involved how to judge the effectiveness of the materials. Students suggested everything from a rating scale (excellent, very good, good, fair, poor) to a ranking from best to worst. In the end, the class decided that each group could use their own rating system but everyone had to keep accurate records of what materials they tried and record observations about how they worked.

Once the procedures had been hammered out, groups set about formulating their clean-up plans and carrying out their investigations. Most groups were focused on extracting the maximum amount of oil from the tubs, and they used a variety of methods to do so. (And yes, we did generate quite a mess in the process!) Cotton balls and paper towel squares worked as absorbent pads, plastic straws and wooden sticks functioned as containment booms, dish soap became liquid dispersants, and pipettes were extractors—all were used in great quantities to achieve success. Two groups, however, seemed to be doing things a little differently.

One group was using relatively few materials and I was intrigued to find out why. I visited with them, and asked them about their plan. It seems that they had read in a book about all the trash that is generated from oil spill clean-ups, so they were trying to use the least amount of materials to do the best clean-up job. I noticed that the other group was not using any of the liquid soap dispersant. Inquiring about their plan, I learned that they had decided not to use the soap because they had read about how the chemicals in some of the dispersants can be unhealthy for the fish in the water. No two groups had the same approach. It became crystal clear to me from both observations and our miniconferences that the thinking behind my students' plans was far more fascinating than the effectiveness of the clean-up. I could hardly wait for students to tally their results, rank their materials, and head to the community rug to share and compare.

The discussion proved to be one of the most memorable learning experiences I have had as a teacher. I acted as recorder because all the students were engaged in sharing their data and observations, but I said nothing. Results varied depending on the amount and type of material used, and each procedure raised vastly different issues as we sought to determine which materials were most successful. Students began to realize just how complex a problem an oil spill is, and began to seriously rethink their plans. Important questions about trash, impact on various animals, even cost, began to enter the dialogue. Students also began to question the efficacy of using a rating scale for evaluating materials. Suddenly, Joey turned to me and said, "Mrs. Dieckman, can we do it again?" Looking around the room at the mess we had made, I wondered what I had gotten myself into, but that moment faded and with a sure nod yes, work began on the revision of our investigation. We made a list of questions we had now, and got out the magic markers to cross out, move, and add details to the procedures.

New elements were added as well. Instead of everyone following the same tack, some groups decided to focus on the trash issue, some added feathers to the water to look at the effect of certain materials on animals, and some added rocks to the tank to look at the impact on the coastline. With a new consciousness about minimizing the use of clean-up materials and the benefits and possible problems with different clean-up materials, students engaged in a second round of investigation. Rating scales were replaced by a record of materials with columns to list pros and cons of each, based on student observations and investigations. Students recorded questions raised by their second clean-up attempt. What I as a teacher noticed was that students went about their recordkeeping with much more care; their observations and records were both more thoughtful and more detailed. No longer were students driven by a competitive urge to be the first to finish or the group to remove the most oil. Now they were actively engaged in seeking to understand a complex problem that would not be resolved as a result of their investigations— only understood a little better.

As a teacher, what I better understood was how assessment works in the inquiry process. It was not primarily about me assessing students to measure their progress or understanding (though that is part of what I do), it was about students self-evaluating their questions and actions, and about students becoming engaged in the process of revising based on their new insights and understanding. There was no need for me to impose external tools for assessment; the assessment was embedded in the learning process and was far more valuable than anything I could have contrived. We were assessing throughout the process because together we needed to think about where we had been and to make plans for where we were going next. In the end, my students' understanding of a complex problem and how to think through, plan, and evaluate a scientific investigation improved tremendously. They learned about how to develop materials and how to use resources to gather information. Students learned that fastest or most is not always best, and that thoughtful inquiry takes time. They learned that revision is just as important in science as it is to writing and reading and learning in general. They also learned that listening to each other and questioning each other is important to deepening one's thinking. Students learned all these things because they had a need to know—they had an authentic question that fueled this journey of discovery. Along the way, as their enthusiasm for learning grew, my energy as a teacher also grew. I guess that's how it works.

References

Graves, D. 2001. *The Energy to Teach*. Portsmouth, NH: Heinemann.

Klentschy, M. P. "The Science-Literacy Connection: A Case Study of the Valle Imperial Project in Science, 1995–1999." Paper presented at the Crossing Borders: Connecting Science and Literacy Conference, Baltimore, MD, August 2001.

National Academy of Sciences (NAS). 1997. *Science for all children: a guide to improving elementary science education in your school district.* Washington, DC: National Sciences Resource Center, Smithsonian Institution.

Pearce, C. R. 1999. *Nurturing Inquiry: Real Science for the Elementary Classroom*. Portsmouth, NH: Heinemann.

7 *Resources for Resourceful Teachers*
Donna Neutze

Recently, while rummaging through several odd boxes of mementoes my mother had stored underneath her bed, I found some of my old report cards. When I skimmed down the row of subjects, I found a grade for science. Did I even *take* science in grade school? What I do remember, however, is the first day in a HS physical science class. There it was . . . the Bunsen burner. It clearly produced a strong (and ambivalent) emotional response: Would I be the one who set the school on fire?

Those first eight years of school science yielded no memories because, I suspect, there was nothing to connect those memories to—no materials, no activities that engaged me, no moments when science became real. In short, there were no science opportunities or challenges that affected my own understanding of life.

Sources

From years of experience trying to help ESIP teachers and preservice teachers locate materials, I know that few of them have time to do the kind of searching necessary. My hope is that by providing reliable sources I can (1) reduce your search time, (2) identify criteria for finding high-quality resources, and (3) offer sample bibliographies that you might find useful for instructional purposes or as model bibliographies.

Search It! Science

Consider Search It! Science [*http://searchit.heinemann.com/*] to be the companion to this book, as well as the best friend you will have when you are seeking science books. Search It! Science is a web-based product, a searchable database of more than 3,300 (and growing all the time) highly regarded and recommended science titles. The database is designed so that its users, including teachers, students, and librarians, can search for titles by combining criteria such as topics, genre, grade level, reading level, and so forth. Users can build bibliographies directly related to their needs, tailoring those bibliographies to teaching concerns—Do you want books that connect science to language arts? Are you looking for titles with strong minority representation? Are you trying to teach how diagrams work in science? Do you want a good read-aloud? How about an award winner? Search It! offers "the books you need at lightning speed." Truthfully, when we paid librarians to do these searches, most took between two and four hours to complete. Search It! does this work in minutes (sometimes less).

The graphic interface is meant to invite in readers—each title includes a cover scan, book summary, and a review culled from five professional journals. Search It! Science is also designed to allow users to search for titles by particular authors and illustrators. All of these features combine to make searching easy and fun.

Author and Illustrator Homepages

Go directly to the source to learn about new books. Here are sites from children's science authors; use them as the basis of author studies, to set up book centers, or to chat with students about the latest books.

Jennifer Armstrong [*www.jennifer-armstrong.com*], the award-winning author of *Shipwreck at the Bottom of the World,* has an interactive component to her site that children will enjoy.

Jim Arnosky [*www.jimarnosky.com*]—Access the travel logs of nature author/illustrator Jim Arnosky and his wife, Deanna. Learn about his newest publications.

Frank Asch [*www.frankasch.com*], the author of *Cactus Poems, Sawgrass Poems* and *Song of the North,* loves to hear from his readers, both teachers and students.

Fred Bortz [*www.fredbortz.com*], a physicist by training, has a science discussion area and an Ask Dr. Fred section.

Madeleine Dunphy's [*www.mdunphy.com*] books often focus on the earth's ecosystems.

Jean Craighead George [*http://jeancraigheadgeorge.com/*], award-winning author of more than 100 books with strong ecological themes, has a Sights and Sounds section, a Q & A section; she even shares a few writing tips.

Gail Gibbons [*www.gailgibbons.com/*], an author/illustrator who writes primarily for young readers, has many books on technology and topics that match the school curriculum.

Linda Oatman High [*http://lindaoatmanhigh.com/*]—Did you know that this award-winning author of *Barn Savers* is also a songwriter?

Bruce Hiscock [*www.brucehiscock.com*]—This self-trained artist often writes about his travels or what he observes in the woods outside his home.

Jonathan D. Kahl [*www.uwm.edu/~kahl/*], a meteorologist, shares his expertise and fascination with the weather through his engaging books and this interactive website.

Kathryn Lasky [*www.xensei.com/users/newfilm/homelsk.htm*] and her photographer husband, Christopher Knight, have collaborated to tell fascinating stories of science from around the world.

Grace Lin [*www.gracelin.com*], an author/illustrator, has a Fun section on her website where she shares some of the correspondence she has received from her readers.

Thomas Locker [*www.thomaslocker.com*]—The photos alone make the site of this award-winning nature writer and painter well worth a visit. His many books are visually stimulating and lyrically written.

Jacqueline Briggs Martin [*www.jacquelinebriggsmartin.com*], author of the Caldecott Award-winning *Snowflake Bentley,* shares activities, ideas, and bibliographies related to her books.

Debbie S. Miller [*www.debbiemilleralaska.com*], a nature writer, provides information about her books and shares insights about the creative writing process.

Wendell Minor's [*www.minorart.com/home.htm*] designs have appeared on more than 2,000 book covers. He also illustrates for noted authors, such as Jean Craighead George and Eve Bunting, and has authored and illustrated his own children's books.

Dorothy Hinshaw Patent [*http://dorothyhinshawpatent.com/*] writes primarily nature books for children, but is also known for her adult books.

Laurence Pringle [*www.author-illustr-source.com/laurencepringle.htm*], one of the masters of sophisticated science writing about topics of social concern, can be found at this excellent website.

Seymour Simon [*http://seymoursimon.com/*], author of more than 200 science books, many of them award-winning photo essays, truly understands children, science, and graphics—a winning combination.

Roland Smith [*www.rolandsmith.com/*]—Read about how he became a writer, examine photos of places he has visited, and familiarize yourself with his books.

Diane Stanley [*www.dianestanley.com/*]—This site contains information about the books, the author, school visits, and a What's New section.

Stephen Swinburne [*www.steveswinburne.com/s.htm*]—What does author/photographer Stephen Swinburne do when he's not writing or photographing children's books? His website provides the answer and much more.

Jane Yolen [*www.janeyolen.com/*]—This site is "intended for children, teachers, writers, storytellers, and lovers of children's literature." Her lyrical texts blend language and science.

Try the following sites for other information about authors including ones that are not listed here.

- De Grummond Children's Literature Collection—Authors and Illustrators on the Web [*www.lib.usm.edu/~degrum/html/relatedsites/rs-authorsillust.shtml*]

- Index to Internet Sites: Children's and Young Adults' Authors and Illustrators—from the Internet School Library Media Center [*http://falcon.jmu.edu/~ramseyil/biochildhome.htm*]

- Kay Vandergrift's Learning About the Author and Illustrator Pages [*www.scils.rutgers.edu/~kvander/AuthorSite/index.html*]

Award-Winning Books

These lists will help you separate the wheat from the chaff. Winners and criteria can often be accessed using the World Wide Web.

ALSC—Awards and Grants [*www.ala.org/alsc/awards.html*]—From this site you can access the winners of the Newbery Medal, the Caldecott Medal, the Laura Ingalls Wilder Medal, the Andrew Carnegie Medal, the Mildred L. Batchelder Award, the Pura Belpre Award, the Robert F. Sibert Informational Book Award, the May Hill Arbuthnot Honor Lecture Award, and ALA Notables.

Orbis Pictus Award for Outstanding Nonfiction for Children [*www.ncte.org/elem/orbispictus/index.shtml*]—From the National Council of Teachers of English (NCTE)comes this list of the year's outstanding nonfiction texts for children. Past winners are also available.

Outstanding Science Trade Books for Children [*www.nsta.org/ostbc*]—Brought to you by the National Science Teachers Association (NSTA) and the Children's Book Council (CBC), this award is given to the year's best science books for K–12 readers. Current and past winners can be accessed at this website.

Professional Journals and Reviews

Many professional journals routinely review books, websites, and other materials that can be very helpful in selecting quality books and websites for use in your classroom. Annual *best books* lists are particularly helpful in keeping you up to date.

Appraisal: Science Books for Young People [*www.appraisal.neu.edu/*]—This quarterly publication reviews and evaluates children's science materials. Available online only. Address: Northeastern University, 5 Holmes Hall, Boston, MA 02115; (617) 373-7539.

Booklist magazine [*www.ala.org/booklist/*]reviews books, reference materials, electronic references tools, and audiovisual materials, it is published twenty-two times a year. Available in print and online versions. Address: *Booklist*, P. O. Box 607, Mt. Morris, IL 60154-7564; (888) 350-0949, *blst@kable.com*.

The Horn Book Magazine [*www.hbook.com/mag.shtml*]—This bimonthly publication has been reviewing books, offering articles, and covering children's books for seventy-five years. Available in print and online versions. Address: *The Horn Book, Inc.*, 56 Roland Street, Suite 200, Boston, MA 02129; (800) 325-1170, *info@hbook.com*.

School Library Journal [*http://slj.reviewsnews.com/*] has been providing information to educators since 1954. Available in print and online versions. Address: *School Library Journal*, 245 West 17th Street, New York, NY 10011; (212) 463-6759, *mailslj@cahners.com*.

Science Books & Films [*www.sbfonline.com*]—From the American Association for the Advancement of Sciences, this publication is devoted solely to science books and materials. Available in print and online versions. Address: *Science Books & Films*, American Association for the Advancement of Science, 1200 New York Avenue, NW, Washington, DC 20005; (202) 371-5464.

Mailing Lists, Newsletters, and So Forth

A good way to stay current is by subscribing to email lists and newsletters. It usually only takes a few minutes to subscribe, and news is delivered automatically. Many of the other websites listed elsewhere in this chapter have their own mailing lists or newsletters. Here are several new ones to get you started.

- Carol Hurst's Children's Literature Newsletters [*www.carolhurst.com/newsletters/newsletters.html*]

- National Geographic Free E-Mail Newsletters
  [*www.ngsub.com/index.html*]
- PBS Teacher Previews Newsletter
  [*www.pbs.org/teachersource/previews/previews.shtm*]
- Random House Electronic Mailing Lists
  [*www.randomhouse.com/teachers/*]

Publishers' Pages

Another way to stay current is to access publishers' websites. Some of them have special sections for educators. Some also have email lists or newsletters to keep you better informed. Here are a couple of examples.

- HarperCollins, HarperChildrens.com [*www.harperchildrens.com/*]—This publisher's page provides details of its latest publications for children and has some special sections that teachers will use and enjoy. Meet the Author, a link to reading group guides, information about school visits, and teacher guides, are all right at hand. You can also sign up for an electronic news subscription so that you'll be sure to stay current on HarperCollins' publications.
- Random House, Inc. [*www.randomhouse.com*]—Find out about the latest books at this site. But to access their wonderful teacher @ random feature go to *www.randomhouse.com/teachers/*. With its teacher guides, author and illustrator information, classroom clubs, and other useful offerings, this website gets my nod for best in this category.

You might want to check the publishers of your favorite books to see if they have websites that provide supplemental information especially for teachers.

Websites to Bookmark

These are some websites that I find myself returning to time and again.

Carol Hurst's Children's Literature Website [*www.carolhurst.com*] gathers reviews, activities, ideas, websites, and book connections for a list of featured titles. There's a section for themes, one for curriculum areas, an author's section, and professional resources; you can also sign up to receive a free monthly electronic newsletter.

The Children's Literature Web Guide [*www.acs.ucalgary.ca/~ dkbrown/*] is a guide to the best Internet sites having to do with children's literature and those who write and illustrate the books. Although there is a Resources for Teachers section, I find that all of the sections are really resources for teachers.

Cynthia Leitich Smith Children's Literature Resources [*www.cynthialeitichsmith.com/index1.htm*]—You'll find author links, bibliographies, and writing resources. You can subscribe to a quarterly online children's literature newsletter. Original interviews with authors and illustrators are a big plus.

The Elementary Science Integration Projects [*www.umbc.edu/esip*]—Stay informed about the latest ESIP publications (that's us) and online course offerings. Find out more about the Kids' Inquiry Conference (KIC). Read the latest issue of the ESIP Network News and join the ESIP mailing list.

e.Nature.com [*www.enature.com*], from the National Wildlife Federation, contains online field guides to more than 5,000 species of amphibians, birds, butterflies, fish, insects, mammals, native plants, reptiles, seashells, seashore creatures, spiders, trees, and wildflowers. You can learn how to create your own Backyard Wildlife Habitat, listen to bird songs and calls, order a free local wildlife guide, or Ask an Expert your wildlife questions.

The Exploratorium: The Museum of Science, Art and Human Perception [*www.exploratorium.edu/*] site has something for everyone. Space buffs will want to check out the Observatory. Sports enthusiasts can investigate the science of sports. There are live webcasts and cam views. In the Learning Studio you can choose from many different offerings, such as the Exploratorium's online exhibits or the 400 reviews of science, art, and education websites.

The Field Trips Site . . . Online Education Inside the Classroom and Out [*www.field-trips.org/*], a virtual field trip site, enables your students to take a field trip without leaving the classroom. Field trips for Antarctica, deserts, dinosaurs, endangered species, hurricanes, oceans, and wildfires are just a few of the ones that are available. Teaching resources are provided.

The Franklin Institute Online [*http://sln.fi.edu/tfi/welcome.html*]—"Expand your knowledge of the science around you with a daily Braindrop." There's a live earth cam of Philadelphia's Museum district. There are interactive exhibits and Learning Resources such as Inquiry Attic and Pieces of Science.

HowStuffWorks—Learn How Everything Works! [*www.howstuffworks.com/*]—This website has lots and lots of information. Supercategories make it easier for you to conduct searches. Supercategory Science & Technology, for example, has fourteen categories, including animals, astronomy, the environment, and space, among others.

Invention Dimension [*http://web.mit.edu/invent/*]—Brought to you by the Massachusetts Institute of Technology, this website features an Inventor of the Week. Search the archives, the Inventor's Handbook, and related links and resources.

K12 Science Resources for K12 Educators [*http://falcon.jmu.edu/~ ramseyil/science.htm*]—This list of science resources includes "professional links, periodicals, content areas, biography, history of science, medicine and technology, online reference and bibliographies, lesson plans, media, careers in science, professional associations, ethics," and more.

Kay Vandergrift's Special Interest Page [*www.scils.rutgers.edu/~kvander/*], a comprehensive website about children's and young adult literature, is organized by Vandergrift, a professor and associate dean at Rutgers University. She writes that "this website began with my own love of children's literature and my belief in the power of both that literature and the children for whom it is created."

Criteria

Thousands of books for children are published annually. So how do we choose from among all of those books? How do we determine what constitutes an excellent science trade book? There is no one correct answer but here are some criteria to consider:

- Attractive format, cover, design
- Interesting and/or engaging topic or perspective on a topic
- Inviting illustrations or photographs that contribute to the book
- Gender equity and/or cultural diversity
- Engaging writing
- Clear, accurate, up-to-date information (space, dinosaurs, medical issues, biology and genetic research need continual updating)
- Quality of content—does the book inspire critical or creative thinking?

Sometimes books find their way onto lists because they (1) address an intriguing or unusual topic, (2) present a unique perspective on a topic, (3) have an especially attractive format and appealing design, and/or (4) relate to commonly taught curriculum topics.

Websites are evaluated using many of the same criteria. The good website should be one or all of the following:

- Accurate and contain up-to-date information
- User-friendly and accessible
- Easy to navigate
- Linked to other sources
- Well-written and carefully edited
- Presented and maintained by a reliable, knowledgeable author and/or organization
- Updated on a regular basis
- Attractive
- Unbiased

Bibliographies: Books of General Interest

There are certain books that work well in almost any classroom, regardless of the unit being studied. In ESIP we are particularly fond of (1) books about scientists and what scientists do, (2) books about observation and observing skills, and (3) books about science and drawing.

Books About Scientists in Action

The following are a few books that will provide your students with models of scientists in action. (For some specific recommendations about books and scientists in action, see Chapter 4.)

Lasky, Kathryn. 1992. *Think Like an Eagle: At Work with a Wildlife Photographer*. New York: Little, Brown.

Lehn, Barbara. 1999. *What Is a Scientist?* Brookfield: Millbrook Press.

Pringle, Laurence. 1983. *Wolfman: Exploring the World of Wolves*. Old Tappan: Macmillan.

———. 1991. *Batman: Exploring the World of Bats*. New York: Scribner.

———. 1992. *Bearman: Exploring the World of Black Bears*. New York: Atheneum Books for Young Readers.

———. 1994. *Scorpion Man: Exploring the World of Scorpions*. New York: Atheneum Books for Young Readers.

———. 1995. *Dolphin Man: Exploring the World of Dolphins*. New York: Atheneum Books for Young Readers.

———. 1997. *Elephant Woman: Cynthia Moss Explores the World of Elephants*. New York: Atheneum Books for Young Readers.

Books From the Scientists in the Field Series

Batten, Mary. 2001. *Anthropologist: Scientist of the People.* New York: Houghton Mifflin.

Bishop, Nic. 2000. *Digging for Bird-Dinosaurs: An Expedition to Madagascar.* New York: Houghton Mifflin.

Jackson, Donna. 2000. *The Wildlife Detectives: How Scientists Fight Crimes Against Nature.* New York: Houghton Mifflin.

Kramer, Stephen. 2001. *Hidden Worlds: Looking Through a Scientist's Microscope.* New York: Houghton Mifflin.

Mallory, Kenneth. 2001. *Swimming with Hammerhead Sharks.* New York: Houghton Mifflin.

Montgomery, Sy. 2001. *The Snake Scientist.* New York: Houghton Mifflin.

Swinburne, Stephen R. 2001. *Once a Wolf: How Wildlife Biologists Fought to Bring Back the Gray Wolf.* New York: Houghton Mifflin.

Books From the Naturalist's Apprentice Series

All of the following are written by Michael Elsohn Ross and published by the Lerner Publishing Group, Minneapolis, Minnesota.

Bird Watching with Margaret Morse Nice (1996), *Bug Watching with Charles Henry Turner* (1996), *Flower Watching with Alice Eastwood* (1997), *Wildlife Watching with Charles Eastman* (1997), *Exploring the Earth with John Wesley Powell* (2000), *Fish Watching with Eugenie Clark* (2000), and *Nature Art with Chiura Obata* (2000).

Books About Observing

Your students will also be observing closely and the following books address that skill and provide rich, authentic examples of this activity.

Arnosky, Jim. 1983. *Secrets of a Wildlife Watcher.* New York: HarperCollins.

Cole, Henry. 1998. *I Took a Walk.* New York: HarperCollins.

Florian, Douglas. 1989. *Nature Walk.* New York: HarperCollins.

Rotner, Shelley. 1992. *Nature Spy.* New York: Simon & Schuster.

Selsam, Millicent. 1995. *How to Be a Nature Detective.* New York: HarperCollins.

From the One Small Square Series

All the titles that follow were written by Donald M. Silver and published by McGraw-Hill in New York.

Swamp (1995), *Seashore* (1997), *Pond (1997)*, *Backyard* (1997), *African Savanna* (1997), *Woods* (1997), *Coral Reef* (1997), *Cave* (1997), *Cactus Desert* (1997), *Arctic Tundra* (1997), *Night Sky* (1998), and *Tropical Rain Forest* (1998).

By drawing an object you gain a better understanding of that object. You will also be working at developing your observation skills. Authors, such as Jim Arnosky, Jennifer Owings Dewey, and Virginia Wright-Frierson, will help students to see the connections between science and drawing.

Building Your Own Bibliographies

I have focused on four areas that many teachers teach—buildings and structures, plants, rocks and minerals, and weather—partly because they represent different branches of science and partly to think aloud with you about how to build bibliographies. Here you will find some of the authors you've come to depend on, as well as some of the newer voices in the field of children's science trade books. The preceding and the following are not exhaustive lists. You may, in fact, read these suggestions and wonder why a favorite book or an oft-visited website is missing. If so, send us a note. We'd love to hear from you (umbc.edu/esip).

The out-of-print problem is real. Books go out of print quickly and often without warning. That doesn't mean, however, that you should give up if there is something here that sounds great. Many of these titles remain available through your local libraries or through interlibrary loan.

One of the reasons that Search It! Science (searchit.heinemann.com) went online was to keep up with what's new and what's really become obsolete. To avoid unpleasant surprises, make sure that the books and websites you are counting on are available before you get to class.

Buildings and Structures

Bridges, houses, towers, tunnels, dams, domes, castles, and skyscrapers are just a few of the different kinds of buildings and structures that you might want to explore. Information about their design, the materials used to create them, and the machines that are necessary to put them together and keep them standing is plentiful. The occasional engineering failure or architectural catastrophe is sure to be a big hit. And, of course, without the engineers, architects, and construction workers, where would construction units be!

Books

Bortz, Fred. 1995. *Catastrophe: Great Engineering Failure—and Success.* New York: W. H. Freeman & Co.   What happens when there is a flaw in the design of a building or structure? Sometimes there are terrible consequences such as collapsed buildings or bridges, plane crashes, or even a nuclear power plant accident. Bortz looks at these types of catastrophes, and how people are able to learn from engineering failures. Author website: *www.fredbortz.com.*

Gibbons, Gail. 1990. *How a House Is Built.* New York: Holiday House. Gibbons' text and illustrations concentrate on a wooden frame house to show the process, the people, the equipment, and the materials that go into building a house. Author website: *www. gailgibbons.com/.*

Hicks, Linda Ashman. 2001. *Castles, Caves, and Honeycombs.* New York: Harcourt.   "Many places make a home . . ." begins Ashman's rhythmic look at the many different structures that are home to the creatures that live within them.

High, Linda Oatman. 2001. *Under New York.* New York: Holiday House. A cleverly created format divides each two-page spread into above and below ground views of New York City. Author website: *http://lindaoatmanhigh.com/.*

Jennings, Terry. 1993. *Cranes, Dump Trucks, Bulldozers and Other Building Machines.* New York: Larousse Kingfisher Chambers.   This book from the How Things Work series employs cutaway illustrations to give you a detailed look at various building machines, how those machines work, and the special jobs they are designed to do.

Johnson, Angela. 2001. *Those Building Men.* New York: Scholastic. Johnson's lyrical text and Moser's images honor the men who labored to build America's canals, railroads, bridges, roads, skyscrapers, and other structures.

Kitchen, Bert. 1993. *And So They Build.* Cambridge: Candlewick Press. Humans are not the only creatures that build, as Kitchen so ably demonstrates in this book that highlights twelve builders that just happen to be animals.

Macaulay, David. 2000. *Building Big.* New York: Houghton Mifflin. This companion book to the PBS series of the same title examines the planning and design involved in the building of bridges, tunnels, skyscrapers, domes, and dams. [Do not miss Macaulay's other titles about various buildings and structures, all of which were published by Houghton Mifflin: *Ship* (1995), *Mill* (1989), *Unbuilding* (1987), *City* (1983), *Castle* (1982), *Underground* (1983), *Pyramid*

(1982), and *Cathedral* (1981).] PBS Building Big website: *www.pbs.org/wgbh/ buildingbig/.*

Maze, Stephanie, and Catherine O'Neill Grace. 1997. *I Want to Be an Engineer.* New York: Harcourt Brace.   In just forty-eight pages, the authors take a comprehensive look at engineering, touching on the types of engineers, the necessary education and training, the history of engineering, engineering facts and feats, and famous engineers. Photographs are very diverse. (See also Siegel, Margot. 1992. *You Can Be a Woman Architect.* Culver City: Cascade Press.)

Platt, Richard. 1992. *Stephen Biesty's Incredible Cross-Sections.* New York: Scholastic.   The book's cross-sectional illustrations will make you feel like you're truly inside the featured structures. Readers gain a new perspective and a better understanding of structures, such as the Empire State Building, a coal mine, an oil rig, and a subway station, to name a few.

Severance, John B. 2000. *Skyscrapers.* New York: Holiday House.   It is possible that this book just might answer every question you have about the history of skyscrapers.

Thorne-Thomsen, Kathleen. 1994. *Frank Lloyd Wright for Kids.* Chicago: Chicago Review Press.   This book has a dual nature. The first section is a biography of the architect and the second section features activities related to Wright and his work.

Wilkinson, Philip. 1996. *Super Structures: How Things Work From the Inside Out.* New York: Dorling Kindersley Publishing.   This book invites you to look inside some of the world's most unique structures.

Wilson, Forrest. 1995. *What It Feels Like to Be a Building.* New York: John Wiley & Sons.   This lighthearted look at structural engineering uses humorous illustrations and entertaining text to show what humans and structures have in common. "When you feel what it feels like to be a building, you can talk to buildings and they will talk to you in building body language."

Websites

Amusement Park Physics: What Are the Forces Behind the Fun [*www.learner.org/exhibits/parkphysics/*]—This site examines amusement park rides and the physics that affect their design. You can design your own roller coaster.

Castles of Britain: Dedicated to the Study and Promotion of British Castles [*www.castles-of-britain.com/index.htm*]—There is a castle learning page that provides detailed information about castles, focusing on topics such as life in a castle, the building materials that were used to build castles, castle provisions, the parts of a castle, and much more. There is also a castle photo gallery, castle preservation information, and some castle trivia.

Cities/Buildings Database [*www.washington.edu/ark2/*]—From the University of Washington, this searchable database of more than 5,000 images of buildings and cities is especially designed and intended for use by students, educators, and researchers.

The Great Buildings Collection [*www.greatbuildings.com/*]—Both buildings and architects can be accessed on this searchable site that often provides links to additional sources about the individual buildings and the people who built them.

HowStuffWorks—Learn How Everything Works! [*www.howstuffworks. com/*]—Find out how bridges, building implosions, backhoe loaders, house construction, hydraulic cranes, hydropower plants, iron and steel, landfills, skyscrapers, smart structures, tower cranes, and hot water towers work.

New York Underground [*www.nationalgeographic.com/features/97/nyunderground/index.html*]—There is a labeled diagram of underground New York. You click on the section that you are interested in to get more information. There is also a photo tour.

Plants

The plants subject category can be narrowed or expanded, depending on your predilections. Consider, for instance, if you want to include farming and gardening, life cycles, and algae and fungi. To spark your imagination, the following suggestions address even narrower subtopics such as composting, the plants we eat, the relationships between plants and the environment, and the basic needs of plants.

Books

Adair, Gene. 1989. *George Washington Carver: Botanist.* Broomall: Chelsea House Publishers.   The life of botanist George Washington Carver, the Wizard of Tuskegee, wasn't always an easy one, as this book shows. The biography traces Carver's beginnings as a slave to his position of renowned and respected educator, researcher, agriculturalist, and scientist.

Azarian, Mary. 2000. *A Gardener's Alphabet.* New York: Houghton Mifflin.   The A to Z of gardens and gardening are gorgeously illustrated by Azarian's woodcuts.

Cassie, Brian, and Marjorie Burns. 1999. *National Audubon First Field Guide: Trees.* New York: Scholastic.   This first field guide for trees uses color photographs and information about shape and height, color and appearance of leaves, habitat and range to help you to identify fifty common North American trees.

Cole, Henry. 1995. *Jack's Garden.* New York: HarperCollins.   Cole's cumulative text describes what happens after Jack plants his garden. Framed, detailed illustrations complement and expand the text.

Gibbons, Gail. 1988. *Farming.* New York: Holiday House.   Gibbons' seasonal approach to farming illustrates how the farms look in the different seasons while also showing how the weather determines the work that is done on the farm, both inside and out. Author website: *www.gailgibbons.com/.*

Glaser, Linda. 1996. *Compost! Growing Gardens From Your Garbage.* Brookfield: The Millbrook Press.   The cycle of garbage to compost to garden and back to garbage is introduced in this book for the young reader. A young narrator explains the process.

Hood, Susan. 1998. *National Audubon First Field Guide: Wildflowers.* New York: Scholastic.   Beautiful color photographs of fifty common North American wildflowers are accompanied by details about their identifying features. Also includes a reference section and a spotter's guide.

Hughes, Meredith Sayles. 2001. *Hard to Crack: Nut Trees.* Minneapolis: Lerner Publishing Group.   This book, which focuses on nuts, is part of the Plants We Eat series; the series uses drawings, photographs, diagrams, fact boxes, recipes, activities, and informative text to describe how the plants migrated, how they grow, their uses, and their roles worldwide. Other titles in the series by Hughes are: *Green Power: Leaf & Flower Vegetables* (2001); *Flavor Foods: Spices & Herbs* (2000); *Tall & Tasty: Fruit Trees* (2000); *Yes, We Have Bananas! Fruits from Shrubs & Vines* (1999); *Spill the Beans & Pass the Peanuts* (1999); and *Stinky & Stringy: Stem & Bulb Vegetables* (1998). Meredith Hughes has also coauthored the following titles with husband Thomas E. Hughes: *Cool as a Cucumber, Hot as a Pepper: Fruit Vegetables* (1998); *Glorious Grasses: The Grains* (1998); and *Buried Treasure: Roots & Tubers* (1998). All of the titles are from the Lerner Publishing Group. Author website: *www.foodmuseum.com.*

Lavies, Bianca. 1993. *Compost Critters.* New York: Penguin Putnam. There is a lot of life in every compost pile, as Lavies discovered when she observed and photographed her own backyard compost pile.

Lin, Grace. 1999. *The Ugly Vegetables.* Watertown: Charlesbridge Publishing.   A young girl thinks her mother's vegetable garden is the ugly duckling of the neighborhood gardens. But her opinion changes when the garden yields Chinese vegetables and a soup so delicious that her neighbors plant those same Chinese vegetables the following spring. (Also look for *Seedfolks* by Paul Fleischman, 1999, New York: HarperCollins; and *Wanda's Roses* by Pat Brisson, 2000, Honesdale: Boyds Mills Press.) Author website: *www.gracelin.com*.

Maass, Robert. 1998. *Garden*. New York: Henry Holt and Co.   No two gardens are alike, as Maass illustrates beautifully with his striking photographs.

Meltzer, Milton. 1998. *Food: How We Hunt and Gather It, How We Grow and Eat It, How We Buy and Sell It, How We Preserve and Waste It, and How Some Have Too Much and Others Have Too Little of It*. Brookfield: The Millbrook Press.   The title sums up this in-depth look at food, past and present.

Paladino, Catherine. 1999. *One Good Apple: Growing Our Food for the Sake of the Earth*. New York: Houghton Mifflin.   Paladino's book examines food from a different angle as it focuses on issues related to organic farming, the dangers of pesticides, and pesticide-free living.

Pfeffer, Wendy. 1997. *A Log's Life*. New York: Simon & Schuster.   You'll be amazed by Brickman's realistic illustrations and Pfeffer's lyrical description of the life cycle of a tree.

Rockwell, Anne. 1999. *One Bean*. New York: Walker & Company. Follow along with the young characters in this book as they observe, firsthand, the life cycle of one bean. (For more on plant development, try *From Seed to Plant* by Gail Gibbons, 1991, New York: Holiday House, and *How a Seed Grows* by Helen J. Jordan, 2000, New York: HarperCollins.)

Websites

Careers in Botany: A Guide to Working with Plants [*www.botany.org/bsa/careers/index.html*]—This online pamphlet from the Botanical Society of America looks at the careers and opportunities in the area of plant science.

Composting in Schools [*www.cfe.cornell.edu/compost/schools.html*]—From Cornell University, this site focuses on composting in schools. It answers questions such as Why compost? How do you get started? How long does it take?

e.Nature.com [*www.enature.com*]—This site has online field guides for plants, trees, and wildflowers.

The Food Resource: Plant Foods [*www.orst.edu/food-resource/p.html*]—
Choose from the list of cereals, fruits, grains, seeds, and vegetables.
You'll get answers to some frequently asked questions, links,
images, and references about the particular food you have selected.

HowStuffWorks—Learn How Everything Works! [*www.howstuffworks.
com/*]—Learn how composting works.

Kidsgardening.com [*www.kidsgardening.com*]—There are online courses
for teachers, gardening Q&A, garden grant opportunities, articles,
and ideas for gardening with your students.

NEARCTICA (The Natural World of North America) [*www.nearctica.
com/*]—Gardening pests, natural gardening, trees, and wildflowers
are some of the popular topics that are touched on at this website.

Rocks and Minerals

Though the unit is titled rocks and minerals, you'll be touching on much,
much more if you introduce some of these titles. Perhaps you'll begin
with some books on rock collecting, classification, and physical properties. Maybe your focus will be on natural processes such as weathering,
erosion, global warming, mountain building, volcanoes, and earthquakes. The sources and uses of rocks and minerals may be of interest, or
what about concentrating on caves or crystals? These topics, and many
more, are covered in the following.

Books

Baylor, Byrd. 1974. *Everybody Needs a Rock*. New York: Atheneum Books
for Young Readers. "If you can, go to a mountain made out of
nothing but a hundred million small shiny beautiful roundish rocks.
But if you can't, any place will do. Even an alley, Even a sandy
road." That is the first of ten rules that the author shares about how
to find your own special rock.

Curlee, Lynn. 1999. *Rushmore*. New York: Scholastic. Details abound
in this tribute to the patriotic monument. Curlee presents the story
of Mt. Rushmore from its inception to its completion.

Hooper, Meredith. 1996. *The Pebble in My Pocket: A History of Our Earth*.
New York: Viking. In her history of the earth, Hooper takes readers back 480 million years and moves through the geological time
periods to track the path of one little pebble.

Hurst, Carol Otis. 2001. *Rocks in His Head*. New York: HarperCollins.
When people said Hurst's father had rocks in his head, they weren't
wrong about this man whose lifelong love of rocks eventually led to
a job at the Springfield Museum of Science.

Kittinger, Jo S. 1997. *A Look at Rocks: From Coal to Kimberlite*. Danbury: Franklin Watts.   Although this book touches on rock collecting, the real strengths are the numerous visual presentations and textual information pertaining to the three categories of rock. (For younger readers, try *Let's Go Rock Collecting* by Roma Gans, 1997, New York: HarperCollins.)

Kramer, Stephen. 1995. *Caves*. Minneapolis: Lerner Publishing Group. This book defines what a cave is, describes various types of caves, explores cave life, provides information about cave safety, and addresses proper caving behavior.

Lauber, Patricia. 1986. *Volcano: The Eruption and Healing of Mount St. Helens*. New York: Simon & Schuster.   This Newbery Honor Book tells the story of *Mount St. Helens* through a successful blend of beautiful photographs and outstanding text. (Another winning volume on volcanoes is *Volcanoes* by Seymour Simon, 1988, New York: Morrow/Avon.)

McNulty, Faith. 1979. *How to Dig a Hole to the Other Side of the World*. New York: HarperCollins.   What does it take to dig a hole to the other side of the world and what will you find along the way? McNulty explores the possibilities, presenting information in a manner that mingles lighthearted humor with facts.

Minor, Wendell. 1998. *Grand Canyon*. New York: Scholastic.   You'll gain a unique perspective of the Grand Canyon from the lyrical text and watercolor paintings of artist Wendell Minor.

Patent, Dorothy Hinshaw. 2000. *Shaping the Earth*. New York: Houghton Mifflin.   The earth has changed dramatically over 4.5 billion years. Patent investigates those forces, including humans, which have helped to bring about those changes. Author website: *http://dorothyhinshawpatent.com/*.

Peters, Lisa Westberg. 1990. *The Sun, the Wind, and the Rain*. New York: Henry Holt.   "This is the story of two mountains. The earth made one. Elizabeth in her yellow sun hat made the other." The book features side-by-side narration and illustrations to show how the earth makes a mountain and how similar the process is to that experienced by young Elizabeth as she made her mountain, on the beach, out of sand.

Ray, Mary Lyn. 1996. *Mud*. New York: Harcourt, Inc.   You can almost hear the "squish, squck, sop, splat, slurp" of the mud. (Also look for *Mud Matters* by Jennifer Owings Dewey, 1998, Tarrytown: Marshall Cavendish.)

Ricciuti, Edward R. 1998. *National Audubon Society First Field Guide: Rocks and Minerals.* New York: Scholastic.   This first field guide focuses on fifty common rocks and minerals and provides more limited information on 120 others. The guide details the properties, colors, and environment for each mineral and rock as well as color photos. (In addition, there's *Rocks & Minerals* by R. F. Symes, 2000, New York: Dorling Kindersley Publishing.)

Simon, Seymour. 1994. *Mountains.* New York: Morrow/Avon.   Simon's exquisite descriptions measure up to the book's outstanding photographs of some of the most majestic mountains in the world.

Symes, R. F., and Roger Harding. 2000. *Crystal & Gem.* New York: Dorling Kindersley Publishing.   One of the strengths of this book is the numerous color photographs of the crystals which are each accompanied by tidbits of information, including where the crystal is found, how it is formed, its range of color, and its uses.

Websites

Earthprints Interactive Photo Gallery [*www.earthprints.net/gallery/*]—This virtual field trip will change the way you think about, and see, ordinary rocks.

The Field Trips Site . . . Online Education Inside the Classroom and Out [*www.field-trips.org/*]—Take a virtual field trip to learn about volcanoes.

HowStuffWorks—Learn How Everything Works! [*www.howstuffworks.com/*]—Learn how earthquakes work, how volcanoes work, and how diamonds work.

Smithsonian Institution, National Museum of Natural History, Department of Mineral Sciences [*www.nmnh.si.edu/minsci/*]—The Department of Mineral Sciences is "dedicated to the study of minerals, gems, rocks, volcanoes, and meteors: their origin and evolution." You'll want to check out the photo galleries.

U.S. Geological Survey Geologic Information [*www.geology.usgs.gov/index.shtml*]—With sections pertaining to earthquakes, volcanoes, landslides, earth surface dynamics, mapping, minerals, and energy, you'll have lots of reasons to visit. There's also a Learning Web at *www.usgs.gov/education/*.

Volcano World [*http://volcano.und.nodak.edu/*]—Brought to you by the University of North Dakota, this site lets you look at the earth's volcanoes, and some volcanoes that are out of this world! It also has teaching and learning resources.

Weather

Humorist Kin Hubbard is credited with having said, "Don't knock the weather; nine-tenths of the people couldn't start a conversation if it didn't change once in a while." You'll have plenty to say after surveying this wide selection of weather-related topics, including books and websites about the seasons, rain, snow, storms, fog, weather prediction, and weather instruments. You'll also find information about natural disasters such as avalanches, droughts, floods, hurricanes, tornadoes, and blizzards.

Books

Branley, Franklyn M. 1997. *Down Comes the Rain*. New York: HarperCollins.   What are clouds made of? Why does it sometimes drizzle, while at other times it pours? What is water vapor? Find out in Branley's look at the water cycle.

Elsom, Derek. 1997. *Weather Explained: A Beginner's Guide to the Elements*. New York: Henry Holt and Co.   Elsom's book examines the how and why of weather, explains weather extremes, looks at meteorology and weather instruments, and explores the world's changing climate. Photographs, drawings, and diagrams are a plus.

George, Jean Craighead. 1993. *Dear Rebecca, Winter Is Here*. New York: HarperCollins.   In a lyrical letter to her granddaughter, George reflects on the world of winter. Author website: *http://jeancraigheadgeorge.com/*.

Gibbons, Gail. 1990. *Weather Words and What They Mean*. New York: Holiday House.   In this basic introduction to weather, Gibbons illustrates and explains some fundamental weather words. Author website: *www.gailgibbons.com/*.

Kahl, Jonathan D. 1996. *Weather Watch: Forecasting the Weather*. Minneapolis: Lerner Publishing Group.   A good introduction to forecasting, the book provides information about meteorologists, weather instruments, weather patterns, and forecasting. Author website: *www.uwm.edu/~kahl/*.

———. 1998. *National Audubon Society First Field Guide: Weather*. New York: Scholastic.   This first field guide to weather provides descriptions, information about season and range, and colorful photographs for fifty different kinds of weather conditions. Author website: *www.uwm.edu/~kahl/*.

Lauber, Patricia. 1996. *Hurricanes: Earth's Mightiest Storms*. New York: Scholastic.   The photographs and text in Lauber's book combine to present a realistic look at one of nature's most damaging weather disasters.

Lyon, George Ella. 1990. *Come a Tide*. New York: Scholastic, Inc. Grandma predicts the tide will come and when it does, boy does it ever. The resulting flood drives the family out of their house to find safety at Grandma's house on the hill, in this whimsical look at spring floods.

Martin, Jacqueline Briggs. 1998. *Snowflake Bentley*. New York: Houghton Mifflin.   The Caldecott Medal-winning book is a biography of Wilson Bentley, a man whose childhood observation of snow and fascination with snowflakes developed into a lifelong study of snow crystals. Author website: *www.jacquelinebriggsmartin.com*.

Murphy, Jim. 2000. *Blizzard: The Storm That Changed America*. New York: Scholastic.   Murphy's multiple award-winning narrative, a powerful story that is told from multiple perspectives, has been described as stellar nonfiction. The well-crafted text, which drew from and features primary sources, such as period newspaper articles, letters, journals, and archived photographs, will be a sure hit.

Simon, Seymour. 1989. *Storms*. New York: Morrow/Avon.   The photographs are simply electric in Simon's photo-essay about storms. (For other weather titles by Simon, see *Tornadoes*, 2001, New York: HarperCollins; *Weather*, 2000, New York: Morrow/Avon; and *Lightning*, 1999, New York: Morrow/Avon. Author website: *http://seymoursimon.com/*.

———. 1996. *Spring Across America*. New York: Hyperion Books. "Spring sweeps up the American continent like an incoming ocean tide." So what does spring in America look like? As Simon shows and explains, spring in America means many different things. (Also see Simon's *Winter Across America*, 1994, New York: Hyperion Books; and *Autumn Across America*, 1993, New York: Hyperion Books.) Author website: *http://seymoursimon.com/*.

Singer, Marilyn. 2000. *On the Same Day in March: A Tour of the World's Weather*. New York: HarperCollins.   If you could pick just one day in March, and travel to different places around the world, you would experience a wide range of weather conditions. This book examines some of the places, and weather, that you might experience if you were able to take a same-day tour of the world's weather.

Yolen, Jane. 2001. *Once Upon Ice and Other Frozen Poems*. Honesdale: Boyds Mills Press.   Various writers reflected on Jason Stemple's ice photographs and wrote the frozen poems in this book. A note from Yolen reads, "Now it is your turn—to read, to look at the images, and perhaps to write your *own* poems. Author website: *www.janeyolen.com/*.

Websites

The Federal Emergency Management Agency: FEMA for Kids
    [*www.fema.gov/kids/index.html*]—The information on this site is
    aimed especially toward children and is meant to help them learn
    what to do in case a disaster strikes. There is also a special section
    for teachers and parents.

The Field Trips Site . . . Online Education Inside the Classroom and Out
    [*http://www.field-trips.org/*]—Take a virtual field trip to learn about
    tornadoes or hurricanes.

Franklin's Forecast [*http://sln.fi.edu/weather/index.html*]—There are direc-
    tions for making various types of weather instruments, definitions
    of weather terms, instructions on how to read radar images, career
    connections, and other weather data on this website from the
    Franklin Institute.

HowStuffWorks—Learn How Everything Works! [*www.howstuffworks.
    com/*]—Visit this site to find out how floods work, how hurricanes
    work, how lightning works, how snowmakers work, how tornadoes
    work, and how the forces of nature work.

The Weather Channel [*www.weather.com/*]—Learn how weather can
    affect your health, change your travel plans, or impact your garden.
    Find your local weather or see what the weather is like on the
    other side of the world.

Weather Dude: Meteorology Made Simple for Kids, Parents, and
    Teachers [*www.wxdude.com/*]—Meteorologist Nick Walker presents
    his favorite weather resource materials. There's also an online book
    titled *Weather Basics*.

Wilson Snowflake Bentley—Photographer of Snowflakes
    [*http://snowflakebentley.com/*]—Learn more about the man who was
    the first person to photograph a single snowflake and see some of
    his snow crystal images.

Conclusion

The hope for this chapter is that you will enjoy the wealth of selections that
await you. The books here represent the authentic voices of scientists and
people who find science interesting and care about making science lively for
young readers. To encourage student choice and autonomy, let children
pick out titles from among a large selection. (Often public libraries have special lending policies for teachers—you don't need to go broke buying books
although, admittedly, this is an occupational hazard!). To foster that sense
of community, read aloud to the class and spend time talking together about
the books you have introduced. These books and websites are sure to make
the science you teach more lively and definitely more memorable.

8 *Looking Both Ways*

Wendy Saul

Listening to educational pundits describe elementary school teachers I feel a queasy déjà vu. The language, as well as the strategies for improvement, are uncomfortably reminiscent of those employed by special education folks as they discuss their client population—children who are *at risk* or who have already failed. The approach adopted, in both cases, is built on the identification of deficiencies—to focus in on what a learner cannot do and to teach those skills that are missing.

There is, in fact, a real problem in teacher education just as there is in the case of younger students struggling to learn. But, too often, this large and pressing challenge is stated in terms that imply a limited set of solutions. For example, when the problem is framed as "elementary teachers lack subject-matter competence," the obvious solution, from a university perspective, is to require more university courses. Similarly, the statement "elementary teachers need more methods" generally leads to inservice workshops offered by school districts. Just as the reading teacher who conceptualizes the problem as "John needs work in phonics" fixates on what John doesn't know, the lion's share of national efforts to improve teaching is basically *compensatory*, focusing on what teachers don't know and can't do.

This, of course, is not a one-way street. Teachers who are worried that their jobs will be taken away or that their schools will be shut down for not having met standards, end up begging for the very strategies compensatory programs employ. Comments such as "Just tell me what you want me to do and I'll do it," which, on the surface, appear to be a cooperative plea for direction, lead school systems to develop curricula that require a minimum of decision making on the part of practitioners. The trouble is that this passive stance, sometimes hailed by insecure teachers, fosters a sense of disengagement. Even in the best inquiry-oriented, teacher training programs, involving lots of active participation, cooperative grouping, and so forth, teacher/participants are rarely encouraged to go beyond the ideas and strategies being modeled for them.

In teacher education circles these days, most talk focuses on articulated standards and performance-based measures; very little time is spent considering what initiating events make further study and engagement seem meaningful and worthwhile to practitioners. This chapter describes work undertaken by a National Science Foundation-funded program known as the Elementary Science Integration Project (ESIP). Like other projects that foster the growth of community, it assumes that teachers are not a homogeneous lot and that change must grow from our current passions, fears, interests, and curiosities. In this sense, even struggling educators can be viewed as teachers of promise rather than at-risk teachers.

Ways In

Jeanne: Teacher Research and Life Choices

Although Jeanne Reardon had taught both ESS and SCIS units, it was her work with science trade books that I found most exciting. She used a piece entitled "Children, Science and . . . Books? A Teacher Explains" to make apparent the kinds of connections she helps her students to forge (Reardon 1992). In so doing, she recognized what in science attracts her—its logic and beauty. Although Jeanne had a fairly strong science background, she had heretofore not given the kind of invested and inventive thought to science that marks her work in language arts.

It was one of those sudden storms. The sky darkened and raindrops beat against the window of Jeanne Reardon's first-grade classroom. Jeanne had never been a teacher to ignore such an event; in other years, she would have taken out a poem or rhythm instruments to help mark and celebrate the incident. But that year Jeanne had been working with an action research project focused on science, and her own interest led her to ask students about the physical phenomena at hand.

In recalling that first attempt to bring more science into her classroom (see Chapter 2), she reached back to a memory of herself as a child sitting at the living room window in Michigan, watching raindrops roll down the glass—"Which drop would hit the bottom first? Which drops were likely to stream together and form giant drops? What in the initial splat makes the drops splinter as they do?"

As the children stand at the rainy classroom windows, gazing across the storm-drenched courtyard, the teacher listens to their chatter. How can she begin the discussion of how drops work? Perhaps by noting the difference between looking at glass and looking *through* glass.

The rain dies down, but a genuine interest in "doing this another time" remains. Here, Jeanne poses a question: "If we want to study drops again, do we have to wait for another storm?" This is a real science question—scientists seeking to establish controlled experiments regularly deal with such problems.

The study of drops continues for the entire school year. Children invent strategies for replicating the phenomena they wish to study: one blows water through a straw at a piece of plexiglass; another drops water in front of a fan. Eventually several children move to the study of the way liquids run down other surfaces. The styrofoam cafeteria trays are finally put to good use—children notice that on days when pizza or greasy foods are served, the water runs down differently than it did on a pancakes-with-syrup day. Students ask their own questions and keep track of their work in journals. They share insights and learn how to doubt one another. As a class, they test waterproof materials. Surely any advocate of inquiry science would be impressed with the work taking place in this classroom.[1]

About Jeanne . . . She is an experienced and talented teacher, a graduate of a small, select, liberal arts college, whose teacher-research in language arts is well-regarded both regionally and nationally.[2] What drives her interest in literacy, her interest in any subject matter really, is a passion for social justice . . . "Language seemed like the most powerful gift to give children from families with little economic or political power." I share Jeanne's desire to redress social imbalances; we have been friends for years. In part because of that friendship, and in part because the subject matter she introduced was less important than the children she studied, Jeanne decided to employ her "self-reflective" and "kidwatching" skills (Goodman 1978) in the interest of science by participating in our ESIP community.

What finally brought Jeanne squarely to the science table was a question, her own question: "What counts as evidence for my first graders?" She developed this question by listening carefully to practicing scientists and recognizing that evidence is absolutely key to the evaluation of scientific truth. She also recognized the ties between this issue and another she has spent considerable time thinking about as a teacher of reading and writing: "How are people convinced? What makes a piece of writing persuasive?" Those with a political bent will also recognize the way this interest in persuasion is essentially connected with the concept of power.

---

1 It is interesting to note that although a unit comparing states of matter (solids, liquids, and gases) is often a topic in elementary school science, liquids per se are rarely explored.

2 See, for instance, S. Jeanne Reardon, "The Development of Critical Readers: A Look Into the Classroom," The New Advocate, ed. Joel Taxel (Boston: Christopher-Gordon, 1988) 1.1: 52-61; and S. Jeanne Reardon, "A Collage of Assessment and Evaluation from Primary Classrooms," Assessment and Evaluation in Whole Language Programs. Ed. Bill Harp (Norwood: Christopher-Gordon, 1991) 87–108, or chapters in this book.

Jeanne was not so much interested in fact, per se, but how facts work in science.

Although Jeanne recognizes that the information she has gathered is fascinating to those seeking a more developmental or constructivist theory of science learning, she clearly feels that her primary audience is not based in the university or the educational community at large. She writes for herself and other teachers, always seeking to articulate the decisions that underpin her activities. She also spends time thinking and writing about how teacher-research questions are born and nurtured. Jeanne sees teachers like herself as perfectly positioned to study what interests them most—real children learning in the natural, everyday environment of the classroom. For her, the science is now fascinating, but it came second.

Mary Kay: Science Education and the Second Tier

Mary Kay, an advocate of experiential learning, found certain pieces of the second-grade science curriculum problematic.

> With the butterfly unit (as compared to the unit on batteries and bulbs), I have a lot of qualms. I feel like I'm giving them so much information, there's so little time or opportunity for them to investigate. They're doing a lot of observing, but I'm the one really focusing their observations, really focusing them, and almost giving it to them, and many times simply giving it to them. They're supposed to be looking at the caterpillar's body and seeing how many segments there are. Well, that's just . . . with all the bristles they can't count and they're not allowed to touch, so I tell them and give them a blown-up picture and we look at that picture. And I feel like they have to have faith in me that that blown-up picture is really a caterpillar, because the picture and the caterpillar don't really look alike.

As an ESIP participant, Mary Kay took this discomfort as a signal, and began looking at the butterfly unit her school district requires. Her systematic observations of children dovetailed with a content-based interest in the principles of environmental science and biology. This teacher realized that her students needed to see the life-cycle process again and again to appreciate and understand its importance. She sought a way to augment the standard curriculum.

> Mealworms help bring the life-cycle concept together in a much better way. We start with mealworms and keep them around for the whole year. When we get to butterflies, the children seem to understand in a way they didn't without the mealworms. My ideas come from working with the kids and learning with them.

Impressed by her work with children as well as her critique of the curriculum, I went back to try and locate the sources of Mary Kay's confidence and knowledge.

ws: What science courses have you taken?

mkh: Biology, the rest were like psychology science courses.

ws: What did you learn in biology?

mkh: Not much, at the time there were lots of pre-meds and that's where they tried to weed them out. It was an intro course that was required, but it was also a very tough course, not user-friendly at all.

ws: Is there any way it helped you in what you do with second graders?

mkh: I have to say none whatsoever.

ws: Then, where did you learn the science that you use in teaching?

mkh: In high school I did take an elective science course on ecology, and it was taught by a woman who was obviously thrilled to be teaching it. She wanted it to be fun. That's where I learned that science was more than rote memorization of facts and that if an experiment didn't turn out right, it wasn't necessarily your fault. When I started teaching, I worked with another woman who was really interested in the natural sciences. She encouraged me to try new things in the classroom, and learn with the children in science. Working with the ESIP teachers has helped pull a lot of things together and helped me to know what good science teaching looks like.

ws: What does it look like?

mkh: Good science is when kids are actively involved with materials. They're asking questions of themselves and each other, problem solving together, and they're looking for proof from various sources.

ws: And what's the teacher's role in all this?

mkh: To be a facilitator—making materials available, encouraging questions, helping kids clarify and extend their questions, and helping them to be critical thinkers when they answer their questions.

In her book *They're Not Dumb. They're Different* (1990), Sheila Tobias describes many people like Mary Kay, referring to them as the *second tier*—the people who

> chose not to do science, not because they couldn't but because in their own view they had a better option. We found [these people] to be confident both in their intellectual abilities and in their verbal skills, curious, hard-working and efficient. (16)

Tobias has directed her energy toward helping university instructors design courses aimed at students in the second tier.

I will claim, however, that the approaches and attitudes she suggests for those working with second-tier college students would be equally effective in working with second-tier teachers. Adult professionals with a holistic, nonauthoritarian focus need a wide variety of learning opportunities available to them, opportunities that in form and content recognize their wealth of experiences, talents, intellectual predispositions, and styles of interaction.

For instance, in response to a question about how she, with unlimited time and resources, would continue her own science education, Mary Kay said that she would like to work with and visit other teachers' classrooms; visit science labs; or take trips with scientists—archeological digs, hikes in the rainforest, a surgical operation. In each case, she'd like to be accompanied by experts who would explain what they were noticing. She would also like to participate in a discussion group composed of both scientists and teachers in which members would react to selected readings. She relishes time to investigate phenomena by herself or with a friend.

ws: How would these experiences provide you with something different than what is found in a good program offered by your district? Is investigating with another teacher, for example, different than investigating in a good inservice course?

mkh: Yes. For example, when Jeanne and I were going to teach batteries and bulbs, we spent a few afternoons testing and trying to figure things out. It was self-initiated play and I was working with someone whom I respect and am comfortable with. It made our talk meaningful and rich.

Mary Kay's action research project was driven much less by a question than by commitments; she believes that children need particular kinds of experiences in order to learn science. To connect what children are apprehensive about with what she hopes they will know and feel as adults, she has reconfigured her science program to better serve all concerned.

Stephanie: On Learning with Children

In the university's faculty/staff dining room several science and engineering colleagues and I meet for lunch. Talk soon turns to the familiar: "What can we do about science-inadequate elementary school teachers?" I find myself arguing vehemently against two solutions—more science classes and science specialists in the school. It is not so much that I object to more science—What reasonable person would? Rather it is that I find the reasons they cite for more science knowledge disconcerting, even troubling.

One colleague asks, "If a third grader wanted to know about atoms, how could a teacher without physics explain the phenomena?" Another, more sensitive perhaps to developmental issues, wanted classes to visit a stream with a teacher able to identify the flora and fauna encountered en route. According to this model, what a science teacher trained in science would have over one not trained is the ability to answer children's questions.

As I listen, visions of Stephanie Terry's first-grade "reel" past. I know that this is a class that any science-concerned university person would find heartening, and yet Stephanie began her work in ESIP with a science background and an attitude that these same faculty members would correctly deem *deficient*. In many ways, too, these professors were right—years ago she was teaching almost no science.

Stephanie is a teacher with wide-ranging interests in literature, writing, music, African American culture, and teacher research. I had heard about her classroom from friends in the Maryland Writing Project, but I never expected, have never before experienced, the kind of atmosphere she and her first graders maintain year after year. Off the streets of inner-city Baltimore, past an outer doorway covered with heavy wire mesh, and down a labyrinth of halls, a dark passageway spills into a classroom where a joyful intellect reigns. There are no smiling "Care Bears," no talk of *adorable* children, just a keen and empowering sense that school is a place where serious, important work takes place and that all of us, children or adults, are fortunate to be present.

During the summer of 1991, Stephanie heard Cachi Canton, a teacher from Central Park East in New York City, and Ted Chittenden of ETS describe a kind of conversation they called *science talk*. Stephanie decided that her children had not done enough with science and that the format described might provide an entry point both she and the children would find comfortable. The children were invited to begin by talking about what a scientist does. Stephanie, with her well-tuned ear, realized that several of her "little people" thought that "sign-tists" (scientists) paint signs, the way artists do art. Yes, her skills as a language teacher would surely come in handy.

One Sunday in late September, on her way home from church, Stephanie found a praying mantis. Whereas in other years she would have turned away from anything that crawled and looked insectlike, this year she steeled herself, picked up the creature, and brought it in to share with her class.

Each morning, throughout the school year, children sat together and exchanged observations and questions about the mantis, and later her nymphs, the mealworms originally purchased to feed the praying mantis, and the hermit crabs who would definitely do better in the classroom than in the pet store that sold the mealworms. Another aquarium was later purchased and turned into a home for newts, snails, and frogs; soon after, crickets were purchased to maintain the life in that second aquarium.

Stories of life and death are enacted almost daily in this classroom. Creatures the children live with, and tend to, have become the topics of their writing and the subjects of their leisure reading. Words like *metamorphosis* and *pupa* are as common and natural in this classroom as *blackboard* and *desk*. Parents trickle in regularly: "Was it true that the praying mantis eggs hatched and that there are nymphs all over the building?" Children discuss where to turn for help in answering their questions; they observe carefully, read a wide variety of books, and have even interviewed and invited in local scientists.

For those in science education, this is an exciting story of the way a teacher, wanting to give her children an excellent education, made a central place for science in the curriculum. For those in teacher education, it is a tale of teacher-initiated change. But for Stephanie the science piece has served another function. As a language arts teacher, Stephanie was, in both her own and the children's minds, the expert. Her work in science has helped define herself differently, as a teacher–learner rather than a teacher–expert, and that, she believes, is what makes her class the intellectually vital and caring place it is today:

> With science I was really learning with the children, I couldn't be the beacon having all the knowledge, all the right stuff. The children's questions really guided me. That's what's made the difference.

Dana and JoAnn: A Story About Collaboration

Dana, then a sixth-grade teacher and active participant in the language arts community, could have been described as science-phobic. She taught the district's mandated curriculum, but did no reading or thinking about science beyond what was required. At the suggestion of JoAnn,[3] a colleague and friend clearly recognized as an expert science teacher, the two joined ESIP in an attempt to look at science across the curriculum, to understand more about the ways in which science benefits language study and language study benefits science. The story of JoAnn and Dana makes concrete what such an exchange might look like.

In one way, their science–language arts collaboration begins with participation in an action research project. In another way, it begins many years ago when they met and became friends. Although I believe

---

3 JoAnn was one of the teachers designated as a Presidential Awardee in science education.

both women benefitted from the summer institute in which they participated, their hour-long, conversation-packed drives to and from Maryland figured at least as significantly into what they learned.

In terms of classroom changes, Dana learned to include a significant amount of science-related reading in her curriculum. She encouraged students to use science literature as the basis for reader-response journals and chose informational literature for read-alouds. She also instituted science book clubs in which children met over a specific title or topical interest (e.g., snakes or dinosaurs). She has invited scientists into her class and seeks to engage children in long-term investigations.

Moreover, she has learned to recognize and build on science in other subjects. For instance, the school recommended a math activity in which students make a one-minute timer. Dana spent a whole week on this activity by suggesting that children make one change in the procedure the manual suggested. If a student substituted sugar for salt in the timer, how would she get it to still measure one minute? There have also been changes in Dana's attitude toward science—on her own, she chose to take a class called Experimental Design, a course she "wouldn't have looked at" in previous years. In thinking back on these changes Dana notes:

> It would have been easy for me to pair up with a colleague like JoAnn and trade—she could teach my children science and I could teach hers social studies. That would have solved my, the teacher's problem. But really and truly, I don't think that's what works best for children. It breaks up the continuity of everything that's going on in the classroom. Also, as a role model, I would be showing children that I don't do science and that that is OK. Also, when I breathe that sigh of relief that I don't have to do science, I stop looking for it in the other things that I *do* teach.

JoAnn has also changed. Although she always used science trade books and science-related writing activities in the classroom, she began to employ assessment and evaluation strategies, borrowed from the language arts, in her science curriculum. She has also instituted her own version of science-related book clubs, an idea sparked by Dana. JoAnn puts it this way:

> Perhaps the major change is that because of collegial support, I feel that I've been given permission to do what I've always wanted to do, to use science as the "driver" of whatever we study. It's also important that if a problem arises I know there is someone next door who can help. Before it was so isolated; we never knew what the other one was doing. It's like team teaching without the kids necessarily being involved in the team. This attitude of sharing has also spread to other teachers in our wing.

> We used to share things. Now, we're sharing the process of learn-
> ing, not just the things we use to teach . . . Because of involvement in
> the project, we take time to share ideas and articles and conversations,
> time we thought we never had. Now we make the time for that sharing.
>
> There's more: Dana's search to find a meaning for science that made
> sense to her, has validated and strengthened what I knew and felt about
> science. Through her struggles I also grew.

The changes instituted by JoAnn and Dana were indeed impressive.
What made their work even more significant, however, is the way in
which their school district took their efforts seriously. This support
seemed to come from two sources. First, they both credit their principal,
Frank Mehm; it's not just that Frank gives them good yearly evaluations,
but because of his own interest in math process, he has been another able
colleague to learn with and from.

Their action research has also been recognized by their school district.
For instance, JoAnn, Dana, and Frank were invited to present their work
on assessment to elementary curriculum coordinators in all subject areas.
In another attempt to benefit from their work, the school system invited
each school in the district to bring a reading teacher, science lead teacher,
school librarian, and regular classroom teacher to a meeting entitled
"Making Connections: Science and the Language Arts." Almost 600
teachers gathered to hear children's science author, Jean Craighead
George, deliver a keynote address; her presentation was followed by
teacher-led break-out sessions.

Rob: A Born-and-Bred Science Teacher

The action research stories reported thus far have focused on teachers
who did not identify with the science community. It seems only fair to ask
if teachers with a strong background and commitment to content-based
science also benefit from work like that described here. So I asked Rob.

Rob is a science educator's dream—a chemistry major with wide-
ranging interests in ecology, physics, and technology—who returned for
teacher education credentials after working in a lab for several years. He
was hired quickly out of his teacher certification program, and his school
district recognized early on that he is a gifted teacher as well as a scientist. He was made department chair of his junior high science program
after only two years, was called on to do inservice work for other teachers, and now leads the elementary and science education efforts at Park,
a highly regarded independent school. Rob writes:

> For me science has always been a part of my life. My earliest memories
> are of observing and questioning the things I found in the world around
> me. I "assisted" my dad on countless projects from preschool through

college and his explanations of how things work were never lost on me. After working in science professionally for several years I began to get interested in what I thought of as the ultimate application of my experience, abilities, and passions in science—teaching.

To quote a music teacher friend, "teaching is a tough gig." When I entered my first middle school classroom, filled with eighth graders, I thought that my expertise and enthusiasm would carry me through. It did . . . for a little while. What I found was that while my students could perform the activities and labs we did in class, they couldn't always express what they had learned in a comprehensible way. Also I found myself more and more curious; I wanted to get a better look "into their heads" and "see" their thinking. With disjointed thoughts zipping around in their minds, thirteen- and fourteen-year-olds frequently find it difficult to express complex, compound ideas verbally. I began to look for a better way.

At this point, I think it's important to point out that my wife is a middle school English teacher, specializing in teaching writing. We frequently grade and plan together and we're always bouncing ideas off one another. I started to "borrow" ideas from her program and adapt them to physical science. I liked what was happening. At the end of my first year of teaching, ESIP and Wendy came along. Just what I was looking for.

I remember that at first most people in the project saw me as a science expert. Frequently, when matters of scientific curiosity or accuracy arose, heads turned my way. But that was not to be a long-term occurrence. What I saw was growth on the part of all the participants. Eventually "language" people began to trust their own scientific insights and curiosities. And I began to change in ways I felt very good about.

I was finally starting to become the kind of teacher I wanted to be. I never questioned my knowledge of science or my love of it, but as a teacher I often felt that there was a better way to teach it. I began to look systematically at the role of writing in my classroom. I began to really see the connections between writing and the other disciplines. By tapping into those connections, my students could draw on skills and abilities that they have learned and perhaps mastered in other classes and apply them to science. And I was getting to know my students in a way I never had before.

Whereas most of the teachers in this action research project, when asked with whom they hope to share their insights, cite other elementary school teachers, Rob describes a broader audience—other science teachers, teachers in other subject areas, administrators and the public. Perhaps it is, in part, because of his comfort with the science content that he feels this confident.

Can This Be Replicated?

There are people who hear about the teacher-development efforts like ESIP and dismiss it as a program for an elite group of teachers. "The group you work with bears little or no resemblance to the average teacher," they assert. I disagree. Although participants are clearly talented, their talents are cultivated and reflect choices they have made. Moreover, each of these teachers identifies herself or himself as a regular classroom teacher; they would be very unhappy to hear that their inquiries and observations are somehow being dismissed as atypical. If we are ever to develop a professional identity, most would say, it will be by seeing the kind of work undertaken in this project as an ordinary, regular part of the job.

In trying to identify the attributes of successful teacher-researchers, I see the critical piece as attitudinal: the best participants are those who believe that teachers grow by learning from and with their students. This is the bottom line. Other qualities are desirable—a deep familiarity with language process, science process, or the processes involved in learning some other discipline[4]; an ability to construct problems of interest to themselves and the educational community at large; an ability to communicate effectively; a penchant to practice with critical reflection; an interest in interdisciplinary scholarship; and a sense of humor. But, these qualities need only be represented somewhere in the group—each individual could not, should not, embody them all.

We also look for participants who agree to make public what they have learned, either through inservice presentations, articles, or the media; this commitment probably attracts and eliminates certain applicants. Novice, expert, and preservice teachers have successfully participated in the project together.

In working with these teachers, project leaders assume that each is knowledgeable and has interests, curiosities, and passions. They are not there to be told "how to do it right"; the environment is purposefully structured to discourage advice-giving. If a participant is willing to invest a year of systematic study in a problem, no simple suggestion can be seen as respectful. What I have sometimes done, however, is to use what I call an *editor's* ear. Generally, people begin by talking in broad terms about their interests or concerns. When I, or any other group member, hears an idea that seems particularly manageable or engaging, we might tell a participant that we have had that reaction and why.

It is also important to recognize the wide variety of projects participants have undertaken in the name of action research. Some engage in traditional teacher-research—asking a significant and clearly stated

4 Although most of the nonscience teachers identify an interest in reading language arts, this year, for instance, we had a music teacher and a school librarian join the project.

question about how something in a classroom works. To help them, the sponsoring institution might type transcripts, supply observers whom the teacher-researcher directs, lend tape recorders, and so forth. Other practitioners engage in curriculum development projects with a clear subject-matter focus. In these cases we, as sponsors, have paired teachers with subject-matter experts and have purchased hands-on materials or books. Still other participants have chosen to look for connections between science and other areas of the curriculum. This year we are beginning a focus on science–math connections. Working with different audiences helps us to grow.

Science and Action Research: What the Future Holds

When I, a teacher/educator, look back over the past fourteen years, I am awed by what I have learned from working with practitioners. There are, of course, the important things one learns from collaborating with any intelligent, hard-working group as we struggle both separately and together to grow as professionals. Those understandings come mostly, I believe, from recognizing teachers as colleagues rather than as students. I am personally grateful for the insights and friendships that have resulted from such exchanges. I also believe that both the science education and language arts communities, as a result of this project, are now more broadly based. That, too, is a success.

At a conference on children's science trade books, someone asked several teacher-researchers what they hope to be doing in five years. None even questioned whether they would still be in the classroom—that was a given. Jeanne Reardon was the last person to answer. She hesitated: "I hope that in five years there is room for me to continue doing the kind of science that I do, the kind that takes time and goes beyond the curriculum." That question was asked and answered ten years ago. Jeanne is now retired from the school system, but we still share the worry she voiced then.

Although I recognize the need for fairly simple and straightforward teacher inservice opportunities, I believe that these should be but one of several choices. Perhaps Professional Development Schools offer an alternative model, where teachers, both prospective and inservice, might join with university educators to discuss as equals the challenges that children and practitioners face every day. Professional development networks offer a different approach in that the pool from which participants are drawn is larger and participants need not worry about their colleagues ostracizing them for taking a different approach to classroom work.

Finally, though, educational systems need to make room for teachers who wish to think hard and are energized by their own, self-defined challenges. If we fail to invite and celebrate the kind of work reported in these pages, teachers and children will all lose and curricula will stagnate.

On the other hand, by inviting reflection, writing, and action research, we can help make schools exciting and attractive places for teachers of depth and breadth.

References

Goodman, Yetta. "Kid watching: An alternative to testing." National Elementary Principal (1978) 57: 41–45.

Reardon, Jeanne. 1992. *Vital Connections: Children, Science, and Books.* Washington: Library of Congress, 1991 and Portsmouth, NH: Heinemann.

Tobias, Sheila. 1990. *They're Not Dumb. They're Different: Stalking the Second Tier.* Tucson: Research Corporation.